EXPLORING FAITH, HOPE, & LOVE

RENE LAFAUT, MSc.

DEDICATION

I dedicate this book to all those people who challenged my immature ideas on love; and my family who encouraged me to not give up. I also want to thank my friends Anita and Mark for taking me seriously enough so that I knew I had some healthy strategies when it came to growing in love.

ENDORSEMENT

CONTENTS

ACKNOWLEDGMENTS

I'd like to acknowledge everyone who has encouraged me in the ways of faith, hope, and love.

FOREWORD

What holds us back from loving?
The pitfalls of trying to work at it without God's grace.

God helps us to live in the 'inbetweenness' of a promise made
and its fulfillment, between our prayer and God's answer.

This is a book that tries to give answers. It speaks in a direct
down-to-earth manner, showing us the things that hold us
back from being filled with love, and the natural transmission
of that love to whoever is around us.

Rene has learned what he knows by believing God's promises,
and wrestling with revealed truth to bring his thinking and
actions into alignment with his faith. A deeply personal
journey shared with searing honesty. His writing has the
power of stripping away what separates me from walking 'in
the Spirit' and each time I spend time reading his books, I am
as it were, reunited with my Lord in some significant way.

Anita Patel.
Fellow traveller

1 INTRODUCTION

The art on the cover for this book depicts love, hope, and faith in the midst of the darkness, with wind and water currents all around; it is a beautiful thing to behold. The darkness, the wind, and the waves are adversaries worth challenging; requiring a solid commitment, a direction, and a central focus of purpose. The light shines in the darkness like a flickering of supernatural love; the hope for the people is the support of a sturdy boat; and the faith is hidden in the hearts of the fishermen in the boat. It makes for a captivating adventure worth taking and re-telling.

In this book I take a look at love, hope, and faith based on what I have been learning from my bumpy journey through the darkness into the light. I have learned that having correct theology on what Love looks like won't by itself grow love. This book became my goal or hope that I pursued with my faith in Jesus, that led to me navigating a learning curve that involved embracing humility which led to love.[1]

I admit it—every time I see a Scripture in the Bible dealing with love I want a recipe that will guarantee me living it out. Who doesn't do this? I have come up with a lot of recipes in my faith journey over time, some have been dropped and others modified, as life lessons accumulate and hope moves me forward.

---

[1] Cf. Rene Lafaut, Dismantling the a Tree of Knowledge of good and Evil Within so Love can Thrive

In this book I will focus first on love, then hope, then faith. The chapters on "Love" are focused on 1 Corinthians 13, whereas the "Hope" and "Faith" chapters are more philosophical but with a God focus. The hope and faith sections offer a framework on how to view reality, and relationships in a way that leads to caring enough to love.

2 LOVE

Focusing on and loving concepts won't necessarily bear deep and abiding love. I have found from experience that if I look for truths on how to love I won't necessarily end up loving people, because as time goes by concepts become more important than "wanting" to love people. Also, if I seek power to love, I won't necessarily love either, because then I may always be waiting for power to love; or when I am weak I won't love, because I complain that I don't have the power to love.

Focusing on love out of caring for people leads to the ability to love. Love is the way. Not truth, and not power. Only love. Love grows in weakness, not strength. It is not about being in ministry and holding onto power, position, and pedigree so we can somehow be an authority on love. We must focus on love: "Doing to others what we would want done to us"[2] in the context of grace, and in this way we will live out our destiny. When we care enough for people we will find ways to love them: no obstacle will defeat us; no lie will keep us; no weakness will prevent us. Only grace will seal us.

Whatever love is, it is either cold and refreshing or warm and soothing; it is not a lukewarm affair. Often sparks are flying in the dark as we fight our way through to wholesome caring love.

I still remember my early struggles and attempts to

---

[2] Cf. Matthew 7:12

consciously love the people in my life after starting to read, *The Greatest Thing in The World* by Henry Drummond. The book starts out by quoting (in King James English) 1 Corinthians 13, the chapter on love in the Bible. The language used for this text was difficult to understand, but better to me than the modern versions I read during that time. The Old English version made love loftier, more exciting and mysterious, and worth aiming for. But it did not instruct me on how I was to go about loving, because I didn't understand many of the older words. About the only thing I got out of the text was that I was supposed to—with pure motives and God's help—give good things to those people I met.

The modern versions that I read of this text seemed dull to me at the time, as though they had no depth, even though I grasped more of the English words used in them. In reality, my heart was hard, I was a poor lover, and only later would I see the words from this text more closely for what they stood for. I would realize that they have a depth and beauty that waited to resonate with the renovations that God did to my heart over the years as I walked with Jesus. At the time, it did not matter which bible version I used of this text. I understood very little of what was said by any of them, because my foundational beliefs were incorrectly laid within my heart. I told myself that I did not know what love was, which was more true than false at that time. The quality of our love determines our knowledge of love whether we can express it in words or not.

Love seemed to be something that only God could properly

do this side of Heaven. And because I thought only in "all or nothing" terms, it provided me with very little incentive to continue along God's path. I also wrongly put the same pressure I used to accomplish everyday tasks in trying to love. We have to co-operate with God in order to love. Love does not come from putting pressure on oneself, and I unfortunately put pressure on myself.

My standards for achievement were set so high that I set myself up for continual failure. Because of this I did not navigate a healthy learning curve when it came to the way of love. Who is going to attempt something that she or he believes is impossible to accomplish? Perfectionism kills love. Perfectionism causes guilt. A better way to love is to do just what is needed to get the job done.[3]

My theology was really poor for a long time, and it prevented me from seeing the good in others (especially non-Christians) I am sad to say. Mine was a black and white, "all or nothing" worldview based on incorrect interpretations of certain sayings found in the Christian Bible. My understanding of love was weak, and I really didn't clue into the relationship between the natural Loves and supernatural love.

The natural loves are: Eros (romantic love), Philia (enjoyment, fondness, and friendship), Storge (family loyalty), and Charity (helping the less fortunate); and then there is supernatural love. The natural loves (which all humans possess as gifts from God from the moments of their conceptions in their mothers' wombs), are good as far as they go, but they are

---

[3] Insight from my friend Anita

lacking in some important ways. Supernatural love is breathed into us by the Holy Spirit when we become God's friends. This new life enables us to love in new, healthier, wholesome, and fuller ways that before were impossible for us to live out by ourselves alone. We get to participate in Devine love. Supernatural love encompasses love for one's enemy, which is impossible to do without God's grace.

Politicians, lawyers, Democrats, Republicans, Conservatives, Liberals, Communists, Socialists, Tax-cheaters, Tax-payers, the unemployed, the working, the rich, the greedy, the poor, robbers, extortionists, addicts, pot smokers, Mormons , Hindus, Protestants, Catholics, Moslems, Jehovah Witnesses, leaders, followers, slaves, free people, rapists, pedophiles, murderers, the proud, the humble, and every day people everywhere all possess the natural loves in one degree or another. Perhaps falling short here or there and excelling elsewhere. But that is not what God wants most. God wants us to love supernaturally: extending, completing, and lifting up the natural loves to where they are destined to reach, only with His help.

Many people are very compassionate, loving, tolerant, and peaceable, but have yet to realize that it was God who gave them that goodness when He created them in their mothers' wombs.[4]

We love because God first loves us. When we experience God's love, some of us can go far and deep along the path of love. Others go weakly or much shallower. We all want to

---

[4] I am in debt to a friend for this insight.

grow in love, be kinder, more caring, more compassionate, and more patient. But how do we move past those things that block us from growing in the freedom to love supernaturally? Those interior things that lash out, or cause us to compromise what we know to be love.

For those who don't have a relationship with God, the first step is getting in touch with their God-shaped vacuum, and drinking in the grace that God pours out through Jesus Christ. This comes from making a commitment to give up sin (i.e. not wanting to love or pay the price to love other people) with Jesus' help, and then to follow the way of love through trust in Jesus and His companionship. He will never leave nor forsake us.

How does it work? Through grace. A relational definition of "grace" means that God loves us whether we do good, bad or have apathy. This means that we don't have to earn God's love by doing good and He doesn't stop loving us when we do bad. This is another way of saying grace is unconditional love. When God touches our soul/ heart we become alive to grace and immediately live for a higher purpose. Those who have nothing to die for have nothing to live for. Willing to die for love is where mature love takes us through grace.

I'm not saying this will give us the inner fuzzies for eternity, rather God's touch gets us through thick and thin as we trust Him, remember His goodness, listen to Him, and follow Him in friendship.

The second step is to forgive those who have hurt us in some way, along with asking Jesus to forgive us for the hurts we have caused others. And receiving God's forgiveness and healing emotionally; not just intellectually[5].

The third step is to pray for humility, and to kill the prideful attitudes that we have[6]. When we grow in humility we will grow in spiritual health and love for people.

Next, we live in the moment, aiming to love out of caring for others by receiving, and giving grace (the way Jesus directs) while implementing the Golden Rule in all our relationships.

---

[5] Cf. Rene Lafaut, Going Deeper With The Twelve Steps for good advice on how to work through forgiving people
[6] Cf. Rene Lafaut, Dismantling the Tree of Knowledge of Good and Evil Within so Love Can Thrive for a healthy grace filled strategy to do this

3 WHAT IS LOVE?

Ultimately God is Love, but to different people love can mean entirely different or opposite things. To clarify what Christian love is, consider what is called "the Love Chapter" found in the Bible:

> "If I speak in the tongues of men or of angels, but do not have love, I am only a resounding gong or a clanging cymbal. If I have the gift of prophecy and can fathom all mysteries and all knowledge, and if I have a faith that can move mountains, but do not have love, I am nothing. If I give all I possess to the poor and give over my body to hardship that I may boast, but do not have love, I gain nothing.

> "Love is patient, love is kind. It does not envy, it does not boast, it is not proud. It does not dishonor others, it is not self-seeking, it is not easily angered, it keeps no record of wrongs. Love does not delight in evil but rejoices with the truth. It always protects, always trusts, always hopes, always perseveres.

> "Love never fails. But where there are prophecies, they will cease; where there are tongues, they will be stilled; where there is knowledge, it will pass away. For we know in part and we prophesy in part, but when completeness comes, what is in part disappears. When I was a child, I talked like a child, I thought like a child, I reasoned like a child. When I became a man, I put the ways of childhood behind me. For now we see only a reflection as in a mirror; then we shall see face to face. Now I know in part; then I shall know fully, even as I am fully known.

"And now these three remain: faith, hope and love. But the greatest of these is love.[7]

An Interpretation

First, a very wise person told me, many years ago, that whenever we try to take something apart to understand it then we kill it. Since God is living, Love is living. We cannot dissect God, so we cannot dissect Love. And that's not what I want to do here. What I want to do is explain how I have come to interpret this marvelous passage. My interpretation here is not the definitive interpretation. Anyone who is further along in the way of Love can easily show me up in both words and deeds.

I will state each verse from the above passage followed by brief explanations:

> If I speak in the tongues of men or of angels, but do not have love, I am only a resounding gong or a clanging cymbal.[8]

This verse doesn't outright say what love is, but it does say that any talk or prayer that is not done with love is meaningless. Love always comes through as pure or clean energy from the heart and mind. Speaking kindly, gently, patiently, humbly, and carefully are parts of loving others and self; "Delivery is just as important as the content of what is

---

[7] 1 Corinthians 13:1-13
[8] 1 Corinthians 13:1

said."[9]

If we are not in the habit of healthily processing our emotions, then clean energy will be hard to come by. Yes, we need to love ourselves in healthy ways, and not selfish and jaded ways. This starts with the way we talk to ourselves and God. The simplest ways we can love others and ourselves are through what we say, pray, or declare: truthfully, creatively, imaginatively, humorously, warmly, kindly, and not judgmentally. Admitting negative feelings to ourselves is far better than burying them and not processing them. But we need healthy ways to process them. We can love or not love depending on how we speak to others and ourselves. Are we demanding, self-pitying, mean, complaining, critical, judgmental (in the name of truth), bitter, angry, or abrasive towards others? If so, then we need a way to clean ourselves up from the inside.[10]

Are we attempting to be infallibly right or appear intelligent, more to feel good about ourselves, or to be seen as in the right, than to bless when blessing is needed? Or, are we gentle, affectionate, gracious, and meek towards others? Treating other people, the way we want to be treated isn't just about doing good deeds but also about how we talk with them (that includes the tones in our voices). Love can also mean keeping our mouths shut. What we say can also become meaningless if our words don't match our deeds.

---

[9] I am in debt to a friend for this observation
[10] Cf. Rene Lafaut, Dismantling the a Tree of Knowledge of good and Evil Within so Love can Thrive

When we don't back up our good promises to others with loving deeds then we aren't being loving. In this case, we become a "resounding gong" or a "clanging cymbal". The choice is ours.

We may think we are funny or have authority to say things to people, but end up hurting, humiliating, violating and wounding them even though we never intended to hurt them. We can't walk away and say that we never intended to hurt them, and so, we aren't responsible. This is being insensitive, cold, proud, and callous in our relational styles. When we cause a car accident unintentionally we still have to pay the price for repairs. In the same way we must make amends to those we hurt, (even to those we hurt unintentionally), apologize and admit we did wrong without excuses. We need to go the extra mile for restorative justice to be fulfilled.

The same is true with personal relationships. When we hurt somebody by what we say, and they say so, we need to apologize and repent. We have to change the way we talk with people, and respect their boundaries and wishes, otherwise the relationship is not healthy.

A very important aspect of communication is how we ask people to do things. Using a tone that is mean, threatening, hard, abrasive, judgmental, and forceful is unhealthy; we can do this when we use angry pressure to get our way. Using the negative energy of self-pity to get our way is also unhealthy. When we do so we find ourselves being demanding and rudely manipulating people.

Moreover, we can still have these negative attitudes or energies in our hearts and speak sweetly to others; the outside of the cup seemingly clean, but the inside all putrid. We know this is the case when people don't see our conversations the same way we do, because they react to our energy not our presentations.

Another important aspect of communication is what we do when we get angry because of what another person did. A bad approach is when we make assumptions that lead to judging the person in question. We may either judge the person before confronting her or him and hearing them out, or we judge her or him without full knowledge about what went wrong. Judging is always wrong as per Jesus' Teachings[11]. Truth telling is the correct way to process our emotions and talk to people who may have disappointed us. But how do we know the difference?

"Judging is giving one's opinion on another person; whereas truth telling is giving ones opinion on oneself"[12] using "I" statements. The former labels, measures, accuses, and tries to use guilt or shame to get one's way. The latter appeals to the nobility of the one who may have done us wrong, and frees them to help in ways we often don't expect. An "I" statement has the form:

"I feel "_____" when "_____" because "_____",
and would like "_____"

---

[11] Luke 6:37
[12] Danny Silk video stream

How we speak with others in conflicts sends messages to them about what kind of attitudes we have. Love is kind and non-judgmental in speech and expression especially when it comes to disagreements or conflicts. When we are kind in potential conflicts we keep the situations from escalating into violence, because we respect and care for our potential enemies as people with value and dignity.

When we see that our approach to disagreements or conflicts breeds more coldness (as opposed to warmth), hostility, or friction, and robs us of peace. Then our default settings when it comes to how we approach conflicts needs to be replaced with Jesus' way of love. We should renew our minds (attitudes, beliefs, thinking, and understanding) with healthier energy. We have choices when it comes to our attitudes or approaches in our relationships[13]. Jesus is with us and if we allow Him, He is willing to reprogram our beliefs and thoughts[14], and therefore our feelings, energy, and attitudes.

For a long time, I did not know what Saint Paul meant when he said, "Take every thought captive."[15] But I found out later. Many times we can have very uncharitable thoughts inserted in our minds towards others. And if we aren't careful—if we don't take those thoughts captive—they will take us captive. And we will speak those thoughts, and hurt those we should really love.

---

[13] Cf. Rene Lafaut, Dismantling the Tree of Knowledge of Good and Evil So Love Can Thrive
[14] Hebrews 10:16
[15] 1 Corinthians 10:5

Words which de-escalate tricky situations ought to be spoken. I think that the kind of speech that does de-escalates volatile situations is what Jesus meant by turning the other cheek[16]. By that I mean He wants us to carry, and let slide the negative, mean, abrasive, antagonistic, accusatorial, judgmental, and manipulative words others may use to intimidate us or get their way with us. We do this when we don't use the same judgmental language back, and politely try to appeal to the person's sense of nobleness when they are attacking us.

We might also want to boast about our achievements or almsgiving if we aren't careful and so lose some of our rewards in Heaven if we don't hold captive such proud thoughts. We need to examine our thoughts, and only say that which will build others up.

Preaching to someone who just did a wrong can easily lead to the person feeling judged, over corrected, and robbed of self-esteem which can lead to discouragement, animosity, and comes from an attitude that says "I know better than you".

Words can be like stones or rocks that we end up throwing. All human hearts can be compared to soils and rocks; some hearts are all soil with no rocks; some have a few rocks with plenty of soil, and others have plenty of rocks and a little soil. Those with only soil are the healthiest and only need water and good seed to bear good fruit like love, patience, peace, joy, and self-control. Those with rocks in their hearts may mean that they have hardened their hearts in some ways,

---

[16] Cf. Matthew 5:39

with anger turning into resentments, resentments turning into hostility, or hostility turning into hatred. People with plenty of rocks are often proud, bitter, jaded, judgmental, and intolerant. It can also be that people vow to not feel anyone else's feelings or humanity, because they don't want to feel their own feelings of hurt or rejection. They are wounded and often wound others; so, they throw stones too. The darkest and hardest hearts still and always will have some soil. Each person has some good soil within his or her heart known as a safe place. No heart is wholly evil. If one did have a wholly evil heart they would cease to live. Because evil requires life to exist, like rust on paint, rottenness on a fruit, or a malignant growth in the flesh. Once the good is totally consumed the good identity no longer remains, and all life-giving qualities cease to exist—hence there is spiritual death.

Those with good soil are more interested in gardening than throwing soil at others. Those with stones in their hearts are in certain situations going to throw those stones at others. The hurting will hurt others; sick people can infect others.

Truth is we reap what we sow. We need to give up the negative, and say "yes" to the positive—all in faith. This will keep us cheerful and steer away the depressing thoughts that we might be tempted to nurse with addictions to pleasures.

When we embark on cleaning up our mouths, we will realize eventually that what comes out of our mouths comes out of our hearts. And what is stored in our hearts? Our beliefs, desires, and commitments that we value and will fight for either in loving ways or hateful ways. There can be plenty of twisted stuff in there.

> If I have the gift of prophecy and can fathom all
> mysteries and all knowledge, and if I have a faith that
> can move mountains, but do not have love, I am
> nothing.[17]

Often, it is thought that God would not bestow on anyone the gifts of prophecy, understanding of mysteries, or knowledge if they did not have a great degree of humility. Saint Paul seems to be saying that we might have these wonderful gifts, but still be without love. If we are without love in an area, then we are without humility in that area. We can covet power over others and knowledge in certain fields of discipline instead of pursuing love. The decision is up to us; are we going to love if we have such gifts? Or, are we going to love even when we don't have the fullness of these gifts? What we do with our lives will eventually give God and us the answers to what we want.

Love does not primarily grow by seeking knowledge, understanding, or truth. Love usually only grows when we care enough for a person and find ways to love them. If we search for how to grow in love we will find truth, understanding, and knowledge but they aren't the real focus, they aren't the goal; rather connection, touch, caring, kindness, and love for people are the focus when we remain sane.

---

[17] 1 Corinthians 13:2

We can also be blessed with incredible faith. But what are we going to do with it? Faith without love is dead. We may be able to believe in the deep mysteries of our Christian faith. But the Bible also says that the demons believe in God, and that there was a time when the demons also experienced those same deep mysteries, although they won't admit it to us now. Yet, they are in rebellion now and oppose God and His elect at every turn. Is there supposed to be a difference between them and us? Yes, love.

5 LOVE AS GIVING

> If I give all I possess to the poor and give over my body
> to hardship that I may boast, but do not have love, I
> gain nothing.[18]

Most people see almsgiving as noble. Few question the
motives of those who give money. What Saint Paul is saying
here is that motives need to be pure for the giving to be
recognized as genuine love. The only motives I can truly
judge, gauge, or be really certain about are my own. I need to
believe the best about other people, and like Jesus taught: to
not judge or condemn anyone.

If we give merely to be able to boast about it to others, then
we are proud, and our actions are not love.

If we are giving money to evangelists, good causes, or our
local church to only receive more money back, then our
motives are impure. Some companies advertise to the public
that they give to certain charities all to increase sales and
profits. It may not be a bad thing, but it is not charity.

Giving money is one of the easiest ways to deceive ourselves
into thinking that we are righteous. When we are giving, it is
easier to point to someone else's faults than to our own. We
cannot love God and money at the same time[19].

We all give ourselves in love in many different ways.

---

[18] 1 Corinthians 13:3
[19] Cf. Matthew 6:24

According to Dr. Gary Chapman there are five love languages: quality time, acts of service, receiving gifts, affirmation, and words and he discusses these in detail in his book.[20] Every person has at least one of these love languages as their primary love language, and if we learn to speak a person's love language, then she or he will feel loved, and likely respond to us in pleasant ways. It is easier to love those who are kind to us than those who are hostile. I believe that it is impossible to love someone who is hostile to us without God somehow granting us the grace to do so. Most people can love those they are at peace with, but loving someone we have somehow grown to dislike takes supernatural love: it takes a change of energy/ attitude in our minds and hearts.

Jesus is the one who introduced the idea of loving our enemies and He himself became our example for doing so. So long as we count someone to be our enemy we won't be able to love them. I have found that when I stop demonizing a person (i.e. stop counting her or him as my enemy), and view them with Jesus' eyes I am more able to love them. If I have demonized them, it is because I have judged them. Demonizing people comes from having a judgmental: "us=good vs. them=bad" mindset that comes from hurt, fear, and pride (or misguided loyalties). Love does not demand from, measure, put into boxes, or hate people. Love sets people free. Someone said that the line between good and evil does not divide religions, cultures, language groups,

---

[20] Dr. Gary Chapman, The Five Love Languages, Northfield Publishing © 2004.

races, male-female, or political parties, but goes through each of our hearts. Reminding ourselves of this truth kills fear, pride, and judging; and encourages supernatural enemy love.

If we are insensitive it is because we have hatred, judgments, pride, and fear deep in our hearts (I know that this was the case in my life for a long time) and it only got dealt with when I applied the stuff God taught me.[21]

Anger is not a primary emotion, but a secondary emotion. Healthy anger comes from being made to feel guilt or inferiority; or arises when encountering fear; or it comes from trauma that stems from torture; or it stems from injustices; or it stems from (moral) expectations when not met. Healthy anger therefore is an alarm. Nothing more. It tells us when something is wrong or doesn't quite fit right, or when something needs to be attended to in our interior lives or our social environments. There is no such thing as immoral anger when injustices happen, but our immoral stuff can motivate our anger. Giving healthy anger an immoral label only leads to getting angry with our anger which gets us stuck, confused, powerless, and a reputation of having an anger problem.

When we get angry, then our focus must be on how to deal with (in healthy ways) what is wrong or amiss interiorly or exteriorly in our lives. If the anger becomes the focus or we nurse it, then it can turn into resentment, bitterness, hostility, hatred, violence, and even murder. These ought to be

---

[21] Cf. My book called Dismantling the Tree of Good and Evil Within so Love Can Thrive

avoided and not encouraged.

When we use angry pressure to manipulate other people in order to get our own way, then it needs to be given up as it is most unhealthy, because we are not respecting people and their personal boundaries.

We need healthy ways to process our anger. We do so in prayer by feeling our emotions, and telling God about them using "I" statements, and not judging, but listening for spontaneous thoughts from the Holy Spirit as we reason with Him about our desires and situations. We will be surprised by the gentle and kind wisdom that the Holy Spirit gives to us to navigate our emotions and relationships when we are open to Him in a teachable state.

When we treat healthy anger as an alarm then the anger will lose its focus and intensity as we deal healthily with what triggered it. Feelings are determined by what we think, believe, desire, and expect. If we change what we think, believe, desire, or expect then we change what we feel. Just because we have anger does not mean our fears are justified, or that we are in the right. We can be wrong and angry at the same time too.

If we have fear and pride, then they will unhealthily motivate anger at times when people don't listen to us. If we are jealous, or envious then we will have unhealthily motivated anger when others have what we want and won't give it to us. If we are slothful and someone ask us to do work, then we will have unhealthily motivated anger. If we have greed, we will have unhealthily motivated anger when someone has more than us. If we have gluttony, we will have unhealthily motivated anger when we are in line ups for food and the line-ups are not moving fast enough. These are motivated by fear. And fear is motivated by lies or broken relationships with God or people. In tackling these we can journey closer to love.

The only way to put an end to hatred is to pursue a relationship with God that seeks to love people healthily. Brad Jersak's book called *Can You Hear Me?* is a powerful invitation to relationship with God that connects us to God and equips us with truth to hear His voice consistently and helps form a healthy foundation from which to grow.

What is the opposite of hate and pride? Caring. We deal with our strongholds of hatred and pride by getting in touch with that part in us (that God put there) that cares for people.

If our default setting for getting one's own way is to become demanding and use angry pressure on others, (stemming from self-pity) we need to change it to a caring for that person, intuiting where they are coming from; understanding how they see the situation. Making the most of every opportunity in a noble way is key to getting in touch with caring, compassion and love.

The battles need to be fought daily and there are strategies to do just that. [22]

Let me summarize what has been said thus far. Saint Paul is

---

[22] Cf. My book called Dismantling the Tree of Good and Evil Within so Love Can Thrive for healthy ways to tackle these.

telling us that our motives play a huge role in determining whether our acts are done in love. Are we going to act out of the good motives in our hearts while at the same time giving up the bad ones as best we can? Love is our decision (it counts the cost and then gives birth to new life in our relationships with God's help). We need to co-operate with God if we are to love supernaturally, because supernatural love comes from God. God has not left us as orphans, He is in the fights with us. And we need to remind ourselves of this periodically, and therefore grow in dependence on God which is always a healthy thing to do.

> Love is patient, love is kind [i.e. warm hearted, gentle, non-judgmental, non-critical]. It does not envy, it does not boast, it is not proud. It does not dishonor others, it is not self-seeking...[23]

What does it mean to practice patience?

When we are patient we can wait for what we want with a good, warm, kindly attitude. Waiting with dark energy is not the same as being patient. We practice waiting without patience when certain forces inside of us say don't wait (or don't remain committed to kindness) with us getting angry and full of self-pity as we wait. The forces inside us that say don't wait might be desires to gratify our cravings, the understanding that it might be easier to not wait (being lazy, and not wanting to pay the price to love).

Our focus in such cases may involve our envy, selfishness, sense of entitlements or unbalanced sense of fairness. The roots of all these are pride, fear and broken past relationships. When we feel more important than others, or think we are better than others, and if they have what we want, we will get angry and self-pitying when we are denied what they have. And this leads to impatience in the way we treat them.

When our anger and self-pity are no longer used as weapons after all the other baggage (like legalism...) and strongholds

---

[23] 1 Corinthians 13:4-5

(like judging...) have been dealt with, then patience comes naturally. Patient-love is not easy to get to if we are a mess inside. We care most deeply when all hurt, unhealthy fear, and pride are healed or gone and we have a completely sane mind. We need to abdicate our hold on being the center of the universe if we want to conquer impatience. This is dealt with by renewing the mind and heart through confession to God, repenting in prayer, undoing lies, and implementing other strategies in the context of a relationship with Jesus where the Holy Spirit leads us to newness of life.[24]

We might want to conquer (all at once) the interior struggles with "impatience" because we see that our conforming to certain moral-standards as being the pathway to Sainthood. If our strategies to attain these moral standards of perfectionism are off base and unrealistic we will not attain such goals. If we aim for moral standards that are not wise, are too idealistic, or are foolish we will land up losing our natural intuitions and there will be a disconnect between our theology and practice. We will therefore invite more falseness and angst into our lives.

Overnight changes are not always desirable because such changes rarely last. Gradual progressive truth, relationship, caring based change, is the path that promises real wholesome and lasting change. The latter is the path that Jesus offers more often.

Repressing our emotions can invite all sorts of troubles in

---

[24]Cf. My book called Dismantling the Tree of Good and Evil Within so Love Can Thrive for healthy recipes on how to do this.

most cases but as my friend Alex writes: "Some feelings might be good to repress [for the time being], because they are dangerous to self and others. That may not be the ideal solution, but maybe sometimes that is the right one" until we know how to deal with such feelings.

Rejection by others or traumatic events may give us an identity crisis that starts us off in the troubled direction of trying to change with the help of angry pressure if we aren't wise. But this can lead to judging, insensitivity, and hatred in our hearts. If we do repress our emotions or put pressure on ourselves, then we must realize that the insight (that we do repress or put pressure on ourselves) alone won't get us to stop doing so.

We must see the lies that we are believing and living out in the face of relevant and liberating truths. But believing real truths is not enough, we need to invite correct, positive, truthful, intuitive, and caring thinking about all matters into our lives. We do so by confessing our sins to God, repenting in prayer, renewing our minds, and becoming dependent on God[25].

If we are aiming to become an unreal saint (like I did for a very long time), then that needs to be abandoned in a careful and wise way (don't gloss over issues) and to pursue being the healthiest oneself one can be with God's help instead. We are all evolving in our beliefs, commitments, thinking, and desires when it comes to how we see perfection. Yes, Jesus is

---

[25] Cf. My book called Dismantling the Tree of Good and Evil Within so Love Can Thrive for healthy recipes on how to do this.

perfection, but we don't see Him clearly, completely, or as He really is without some (or a lot of) static and much disconnection. We can and do trust Him, and He does guide us, but the path is a long one. If we are aiming to be the perfect parent when the perfect parent we have in mind is not based in reality, then we need to abandon that too but slowly, thoughtfully, wisely, and prayerfully. If a spaceship's aim is one degree off its course it will never get to its destination when the target is far enough away.

Practicing: "Love is kind" can be life changing. The Bible says in part, that it is God's kindness that leads us to repentance[26]. How much more ought we to have the same attitude, as God has, of kindness, when we desire change in our children, spouses, friends, customers, co-workers, leaders, followers, and enemies. The way to work this is to remember that when God's kindness is directed to us that it has had good consequence in our lives, so how can that be a bad thing when it comes to us wanting change in other peoples' behaviors or decisions that affects us?

We love because God first loves us! I have found that when I change my attitudes towards goodness and give up judging people, then people recognize my energy change and treat me differently. If we don't practice "love is kind" we will attempt to use anger, meanness, manipulation, cold self-pity and abrasiveness to get our way. If we aren't kind, then we will also judge out of pride, blindness and insensitivity those people we are trying to correct – or change and only land up

---

[26] Cf. Romans 2:4

hurting them. Controlling people is not the same as these same people responding in devotion, inspiration, loyalty, gratitude, love, caring, or obedience to the powers that be or possibly us. Control over people is most often an illusion.

If we are not gentle with ourselves then we won't be gentle with others. If we are gentle with ourselves, we will more likely be gentle with others, but not always. Putting pressure on oneself to love will always backfire. If you put angry pressure on yourself, you will see your patience (for yourself and others) dry up; and your joy will dry up too. Angry pressure kills our ability to be compassionate. Angry pressure can be entrenched in many areas of our relational and interior lives. It will take time to repent from these even with the right tools.[27]

We can be hard on ourselves because of shame (that says there is something wrong with our identity, unlike guilt that says there is something wrong with our actions). If so, we will most likely attempt to "do more and try harder" to overcome what we see to be the source of our shame (otherwise we will "give up"; or see-saw "back and forth" between "trying harder" and "giving up"). The only way out is to recognize and confess to God the lies that foster the "doing more; trying harder" cycles perpetuated by our shame and brokenness. Then, to repent in faith and renew our minds with healthy truth, and to fight the fight of faith by finding, celebrating, and embracing the grace whose source is Jesus the Way, the

---

[27] Cf. My book called Dismantling the Tree of Good and Evil Within so Love Can Thrive for healthy recipes on how to do this.

Truth, and the Life. Then to live out of what God says is the truth about our behaviors, our value and identities, and our acceptance by Him.[28]

Grace comes from God. But we can aim to be graceful to ourselves and other people too. Grace is unconditional love. This means that we love people "whether or not" they do good, bad, or have apathy. This means that they don't have to do good to be loved by us, and they are not penalized by us for doing bad either. This is most freeing.

If we have joy then we won't necessarily be seeking gratification (for ourselves) in other things and that means we will be less jealous and greedy, more patient and more giving and kind to others. Joy is one building block to practicing patience. Joy means we have something to share and celebrate. Joy is God's gift to us that comes from searching for our gratitude, and not putting all of one's energy into trying to get happy. Joy comes from seeing what you already have, and not from necessarily setting one's heart on new things.

Lack of joy is a result of either not having been forgiven or just intellectualizing being forgiven. God wants to restore us by grace (and to feel it). We must deal with our current baggage/ burdens that drag us down, through confession to God (receiving forgiveness emotionally besides intellectually), repenting in prayer, and replacing lies with truth for joy to grow. Forgiveness is a gift just like grace; and they both need

---

[28] Cf. Jeff VanVonderen, Tired Of Trying To Measure Up, Bethany House Publishers © 1989

to be examined, embraced, celebrated, and shared.

If we want to practice patience we need to get in touch with those parts within that care for others (that God puts in all of our hearts at our conceptions). Caring for others is another building block to practicing patience. If we care for ourselves in healthy ways, not just selfish ways, then we will care for others more when practicing the Golden Rule. We won't move away from revenge, retribution, and wrath unless we choose to care for people and refuse to demonize them. We need to value and respect people to love them.

If we want to practice patience and love, then we must start where we are at and meet God there in prayer. We find out where we are at when we have conversations with God. Jesus said His sheep know His voice[29]. Knowing where we are, requires spiritual eyesight and Light. Jesus is the Light of the world. We can't know where we are at unless we have Him shining into our lives!

If we want to practice patience with others and ourselves, then we need to stop judging harshly our and other people's behaviors and motives. Judgmentalism is rooted in envy that is rooted in pride and contempt; that are rooted in fear; that is rooted in resentment or hurts; and are blockages to practicing love.[30]

Judgmentalism is also rooted in wrong perceptions of who God is. This might show itself in attributing a hard, mean,

[29] Cf. John 10:27
[30] Cf. My book called Dismantling the Tree of Good and Evil Within so Love Can Thrive

angry, impatient voice to God when we ask God for advice. God does not drive His children with a whip! God's heart is for us to be set free to love and not to be treated as slaves.

We will not be patient if our foremost focus is us keeping the OT Law (Torah or Moral Law or even misguided ideals or principles). All the Law does is tell us what is wrong or sinful. Trusting the law to somehow help us to keep the law will not work. Our foremost focus needs to be Jesus, God's wisdom and love flowing through us instead of keeping score on what is fair or unfair. A healthy Christian focus is on grace not fairness or unfairness for oneself.

Always focusing on fairness is a trap that helps give envy a firm place in our lives. It leads to judging, and kills giving love to people.

The Torah or OT Law was the "minimum standard"[31] that God required from the Jewish people a long time ago. Jesus' teachings and commands are so much higher, that when we keep them through faith and grace, the Torah or OT Law is fulfilled. The OT Law is about fairness, about people having rights. If we focus on only protecting our rights we will never love, no matter how right our rights may be.

If we think that God does not love sinners until they repent, with us doing the same in such instances, then we have not taken seriously the example of Jesus in the Gospels who was a friend of tax collectors, prostitutes, and sinners. God

---

[31] These words were first coined together by Dr. Mark and Patti Virkler in their book *Rivers of Grace* in the context of the OT's importance and is used with permission.

unconditionally loves us: that means He loves us without conditions. We need to be gentle and see that Jesus is our breathing room from the Law that demands perfection. All that Laws can do is to point out sins, they won't make anything perfect. Love is not legislated, but inspired.

We need to be at rest interiorly. Peace gives us perspective. Rest and peace are building blocks to patience and love. Rest only happens when we are standing on a sturdy foundation: Jesus; and when we believe in God's love shown through His forgiveness.

Jesus is the rock of our salvation. He is the divine Principle: believing, trusting, and resting in His love and power and voice is the key to us loving supernaturally. He does not leave us to our own devices. He will help us keep His principles and maxims and commands in the light of loving people. Without Him principles and maxims turn into cold stone dead burdens of Law that weigh us down. Again, aiming at keeping rules only by focusing on the rules is a sure path to failure, judging others, and being impatient with those not keeping the rules.

If we are in the habit of getting angry with ourselves each time we break a commandment, then we will do the same with everyone else we see breaking commandments we are aware of. Showing remorse or being contrite is healthier after we sin.

If we are committed to the philosophy of: "an eye for an eye and a tooth for a tooth"[32] we basically foolishly believe that a

---

[32] Exodus 21:24

person either deserves favor or grace if he or she is good; or should be condemned if he or she does bad things. This should not be so. Grace is meant for the good, the bad, and the ugly. Grace is not deserved, it is a gift.

Patience can't be practiced if we believe the lie that: "we never or hardly ever get our way." We will always resent giving our time, talent, or treasure to people if we believe that we don't get anything back from them some of the time. This is how self-pity works. Sometimes, what we get back from helping people is meaning and purpose. Who can put a price on that?

Joy in a person is attractive and draws other people closer. We need joy which resides in the heart; unlike happiness that resides in the mind and pleasure that resides in the body[33]. Joy comes from our gratitude, and for Christians that gratitude comes in part because we are celebrating Jesus having forgiven our past sins out of love, and our adoption into God's family out of love, as sisters and brothers of Christ. Gratitude and joy kill self-pity.

Joy and anger don't mix. When we have joy it is easier to be patient. When we carry anger, or are in the habit of using it to get our way, we won't be as patient with people. When we carry angry pressure with us we will land up getting angry about stuff that hasn't even happened yet. There is help for

---

[33] Peter Herbeck video stream from the Internet

this.[34]

When one seeks to learn from and follow Jesus, one will learn how to deal with one's anger in constructive and healthy ways, this is a gradual process.[35] I have found that the more I learn to deal with unresolved anger, and how to deal with anger in the present my ability to be patient has gradually improved. Dr. Gary Chapman's book on anger gives some steps on how to process anger in healthy ways. These steps work, but they take God's grace to work as designed. Often things that annoy us, or anger us or need to be dealt with or that need to be forgiven can only be processed healthily with God through prayer by imitating God in the way He dispenses grace.

God never stops loving us because of our sins. If we do choose sin over following God, then God still loves us. But His love can't get through because we have possibly set walls up of resentment, fear, pride, envy, greed, judging, lust, sloth, and gluttony along with self-pity and anger that push God and everyone else possibly very far away.

When we are impatient (i.e. give up being patient with people) we are not kind (warm-hearted), we are covetous (thinking about ourselves alone), we are pompous and have an inflated sense of our own worth (have unhealthy pride); we are rude (have contempt) and are selfish (not caring about

---

[34] Cf. Rene Lafaut, Dismantling the Tree of Knowledge of Good and Evil So Love Can Thrive
[35] Cf. Gary Chapman, Anger: Handling A Powerful Emotion In Healthy Ways

others). If we have any one of these behaviors, we usually have them all. The root of impatience is selfishness that comes from pride that comes from fear that comes from a broken relationship with people and ultimately disconnection from God. The root of impatience is fear and thinking that we are more deserving than others. A root of impatience is pride. A root of impatience is "I" without Christ! It is felt through indulging in self-pity and angry pressure. It's thinking that we deserve what others have. And possibly hating them for it because of our envy. Perhaps we covet being first in the line-ups at the supermarket. If we do, then we are more than likely going to have unkind thoughts and feelings (such as anger, self-pity, hatred, intolerance, hostility, judgment, and contempt) towards those ahead of us in the line-ups and for the seemingly slow and chatty cashiers. Yet love is kind.

Jesus said it is better to give than to receive. If we really love humanity, we will love our neighbor, and that means relinquishing our hold on being number one wherever we go. If we are following Jesus, then His will is first in our lives. When Jesus' will is not first in our lives, then we are not following him fully; we are trying to do life on our own terms (but apart from Jesus we can do nothing; for He is the Vine and we are the branches[36]). Jesus is only number one in our lives when we are patient with people out of love. We are patient with others when we actively do love people by waiting for them in kindness. We can't love God if we don't love people.

---

[36] Cf. John 15:5

If we are patient, we are kind (warmhearted). If we are kind, we are not jealous. If we are not jealous (we are generous), we are not pompous. If we are not pompous, we are not inflated. If we are not inflated, we are not rude. If we are not rude, we are not going to seek our own interests all of the time. If we are not going to seek our own interests all of the time, we are not going to be selfish. If we are not going to be selfish, we are going to be patient.

All the above positive-behaviors are linked together.

Pope Francis said to give thanks to God for giving others the gifts He has given so generously. Moreover, this truth in dealing with jealousy and pride is more than a principle to be admired and fitted into our theological system of thought. We need to practice it too when we get jealous or envious, because that is where the rubber meets the road to victory over judging people and having victory over our sense of superiority and narcissistic attitudes.

When I used to read the verse that says, "[Love]…does not seek its own interests"[37] I got confused. But when I'm loving somebody else I can't be seeking my own interests because love cares for all people besides just myself, and that includes their healthiest interests. If we are doing something for someone else, but the only reason we are performing the act is because of what we will personally get out of it, then we are scheming and we aren't really concerned with loving or pleasing that someone else. In this case, we are only concerned about what we will get. Love does not seek its own

---

[37] 1 Corinthians 13:5

interests when loving others; love seeks the highest good of those in our power to love.

If we like roast beef sandwiches, but our friend likes egg salad sandwiches, then giving them roast beef sandwiches instead of egg salad sandwiches is love gone wrong when it is in our power to give them what they want.

Love's foremost concern when directed at others is with blessing others with life and the joy thereof. It does not scheme, manipulate, use guilt or shame on others in order to get a desired selfish end or even some sort of justice. "Love does not seek its own interest," means that when we are loving a person we are seeking their best (healthiest) interest not necessarily ours. Just because we like something doesn't mean they will.

Love is not selfish! And Saint Paul is still not finished. He goes on...

> [Love]… is not easily angered, it keeps no record of wrongs. Love does not delight in evil but rejoices with the truth.[38]

What does it mean to be quick-tempered? It means to make quick assumptions and by them getting angry. It is natural to have certain emotions like anger or frustration at times. But to carry them with us day in and day out goes against this verse and therefore it goes against love. We do this by holding resentments or seeking change through angry pressure.

Anger often comes from hurts inflicted on us. It is only done away with through processing it in healthy ways, and that may mean needing to give up judgments and conceit or to forgive and maybe change what we value or believe in. We need to process and work through and accept our emotions, reactions, anger, and frustrations. Every healthy saint did or does the same: they work through their emotions no matter how uncomfortable, and working through the process we learn to love and forgive those people who trouble(d) us. Such a process takes caring, time, wisdom, and grace.

I found for a long time that I didn't want to embrace my emotions because I thought they would take me to places I didn't want to go, but when I do process my emotions in prayer through renewing my mind which encompasses: using

---

[38] 1 Corinthians 13:5-6

"I" statements; repentance; deciding to love anyways; and dialoguing with God, I find situations are resolved with wisdom and kindnesses that I could not otherwise come up with all by myself.

It is true that quick-tempered people are impatient. We are impatient when we say "the hell" with someone because that someone is not living up to our expectations. If someone is not living up to our expectations, then hardness may creep into our hearts and we can get nasty with them. This can further lead to resentments forming (i.e. we don't want to give up our anger and judgments). When this happens we forget that we are no better than those who have disappointed us. When we brood over injuries done to us, we are not treating the agents of our hurts like we would want to be treated in similar situations.

We are forgetting that we too are agents of hurt, and also require patience and forgiveness from others. We too require mercy from others. If we refuse to be merciful to others, we are burning the bridge that would have mercy travel to us from God. "Blessed are the merciful for they will be shown mercy".[39] If we aren't merciful or patient with ourselves, and aren't waiting on (or searching for) God to slowly mature our love, devotion, purity, and commitments then we will be "anger" and "whip driven" and not love motivated. God does not expect instant compliance with His commands. He knows that real change is a process, a learning curve, and sometimes a fight. It is a process that He is happy to help us with as we

---

[39] Cf. Matthew 5:7

renew our minds with His peace, grace and wisdom. If we don't sense Jesus as wanting to help us as genuinely true. But see Jesus' true image (not knowing any better) replaced with a counterfeit based on lies from the devil then we need to read the Gospels and see for ourselves that we have a case of mistaken identity of what Jesus' voice really sounds like. This will correct our judgments and law focused mentalities as we reject the counterfeits and our minds are renewed.

The first part of the next sentence under scrutiny, "Love does not rejoice over wrongdoing" is easier to understand than the second part that says, "but rejoices with the truth." Taken together or in context, what do these mean? What is Saint Paul trying to get at here?

In order for "love to rejoice in the truth", one has to find it in oneself and others. If we are negative or critical towards others, we will always be skeptical about their goodness or motives. Fact is, we all have some goodness and beauty in us. If we didn't we'd cease to exist because God does not create junk. All truth and beauty is a preparation for the Good News of Jesus Christ. This truth and beauty are not only a "preparation for the future" but the steel that helps to build bridges to accepting Jesus as Leader and Savior.

Negative people see the cup as half empty; whereas lovers rejoice in all beauty and truth found in others. The one who looks for the beauty in others, encourages it, waters it, prays for it, and blesses it, is a lover.

People who are negative are closed-minded, they are into putting people into boxes, and they are judgmental. They have a lot of unresolved self-pity, anger and pride. The first Psalm says: "Blessed is the person who does not walk in the counsel of the wicked or stands in the path of sinners or sits in the seat of mockers." Negative people have a tendency to make good things die: first in themselves then in others. God is positive. So what flows through Him is positive life or energy that flows into us and out of us, into the lives of others when we act humbly. We are the branches, He is the vine. His fruit is sweet not bitter! "We bear good fruit; we don't produce it all by ourselves!"[40]

I also believe that Saint Paul is contrasting two ways of relating. The reckless, the heartless, the uncaring, and the unloving rejoice over wrongdoing that gets them a desired treasure in the end, whereas lovers of God rejoice over a certain kind of truth. This truth has nothing to do with the abstract or practical theorems found in mathematics, but has to do with a kind of life. This kind of truth has to do with not practicing hypocrisy. When we are true to God, we won't be hypercritical. When we are false, we are hypocritical. Truth and hypocrisy don't mix. They are opposites. Hypocrisy happens when we judge and condemn other people for the very things we still do. Hypocrisy can happen when we also expect from others what we would not do for them, that we have the power and ability to do.

When we relate in truth and not out of hypocrisy, we are behaving more like God; and we will love God and others with our whole being. When we truly love others, they become

---

[40] Pastor Hugh Walker

more important and have value in our eyes, and we are willing to sacrifice ourselves for them. We can't do this by ourselves; only by connecting with and submitting in gentleness to the Vine: Jesus, is it then possible. This takes humility.

8 LOVE AS SACRIFICE

Love as sacrifice is best seen in the way God loves us.

> Love does not delight in evil but rejoices with the
> truth. It always protects, always trusts, always hopes,
> always perseveres.[41]

Love is willing to believe that all the hardships, all the
suffering, and all the evil in this world, is tolerated by a kind
God out of love. Namely in Him being patient with us so that
He can save and heal as many people as possible to the
uttermost as we see the consequences of our actions and
choose to make healthy changes in our attitudes and minds.

Love believes that God became man so that He could take on
our hardships, and our sufferings to be close to us and to
become our friends. Love believes that the Almighty became
human so that He could reverse Adam's spineless response to
not love his wife to the point of death in the Garden of Eden
so very long ago. Love believes that Jesus came to reconcile
us to Himself. Love believes that Jesus entered death so that
He could reclaim the dead and give us all life. God does not
condemn anyone, but people can and do condemn
themselves by ignoring God's warnings about what sin can do
to us.

Love believes that out of the foolish proclamation that "God
is love" and in Him there is no darkness, people will accept
God's love and receive Him into their hearts by saying yes to

---

[41] 1 Corinthians 13:6-7

His warm invitations.

Love is willing to hope in God's promises until they are fulfilled. Love is willing to endure all things until we finally see God. We won't be disappointed because of who He is. Many get disappointed when they only see the "supposed" weakness of God hanging on a cross. They may think: "What a pathetic God." Many don't see His strength in being able to endure that suffering and to love us even when we ridiculed, mocked, hated, spat, and laughed at Him during His Passion. He became weak so that He could show His strength: that is His love.

Sin is mutilation, and Righteousness is healing. This is the meaning of: "He became sin so that we could become the righteousness of God."[42] Jesus was mutilated in the flesh during His Passion so that we could be made spiritually whole or healthy through His grace by a humble teachable faith. This is the Good News.

The Significance Of Love:

> Love never fails. But where there are prophecies, they will cease; where there are tongues, they will be stilled; where there is knowledge, it will pass away.[43]

Love never fails to be important. When love is important, love never fails to be the goal, it never fails to be the aim. Prophecies will cease to be important after they have been fulfilled. Speaking will cease to be important as far as making

---

[42] 2 Corinthians 5:12
[43] 1 Corinthians 13:8

promises to love is concerned. Talking about love will cease to be important, loving will become the challenge and reality in word and deed. Even the knowledge that we now have will pale in significance to the reality of God and His Love yet to be revealed to those who patiently endure in faith, hope and love the burdens life throws our way.

Anticipation Of Love:

> For we know in part and we prophesy in part, but when completeness comes, what is in part disappears.[44]

The first part of this sentence speaks to the sad reality of life on this side of Heaven. We only know partially and should not think that absolute truth is attainable (we don't see all beginnings and all ends; absolute truth is God's domain because we do not see all the limitations and strengths of the truths we believe). Nothing is perfect or fully mature in this life. Prophecy is meant to point to knowing God. The prophecy in the Bible as it now stands is partially fulfilled. And those who know God, or have experienced Him, do so partially. But there is hope, because the perfect is promised by God to come someday to those who are patient with God. History and time are racing towards that climax when God will be revealed in all His glory to us.

As we grow up in the faith, old doubts will be consumed by new faith, and new doubts will emerge to challenge us until Christ is formed completely within us.

---

[44] 1 Corinthians 13:9-10

Growing Up Spiritually In Love:

> When I was a child, I talked like a child, I thought like a child, I reasoned like a child. When I became a man, I put the ways of childhood behind me.[45]

The inbetween stage from childhood to adulthood is one of the most difficult to navigate. It is often marked by growing pains as we are asked to give more than to receive. Life slowly turns out to be far from what we imagined as children. For many of us it is marked by feeling distance between us and our parents as we navigate the changes, opportunities, and difficulties that come our way as we struggle with authority, identity, the herd instinct, and possibly rebellion. But if we do mature, we put behind us the hurts and discipline measured out to us when we were young and naive.

We then begin to see our parents more so for who they are, and begin again to enjoy their company in a deeper way. The few, who make it this far, get to enjoy the fellowship that results from connecting, caring, warmth, understanding, and forgiveness. By this time they are more deeply involved with loving their parents back. They also recognize their parents' love for what it is.

What is said above about human relationships can also be said about those who are in relationship with God. Not everyone will work on his or her relationship with God through the difficult times. Those who do persevere discover new depths, insights, connections, and fellowship with God

---

[45] 1 Corinthians 13:11

that are all gifts of God's grace that are likely unwrapped through pain. This new life has nothing to do with stagnancy which is more a trait belonging to closed-minded people without real faith.

Making Maps Of Love:

We are all given road maps or world-views as we first start out. They are usually impressed onto our minds by our parents, teachers, and friends whether they are well meaning or not. Even our enemies do have a say in how our maps are going to turn out.

Some of us burn the road maps that we inherit and pursue something else entirely different. This can be either good or bad depending on whether we do so with wisdom or not.

All of us covet different things as we grow and change. All of us want to avoid different things as we grow and change. Many covet pleasure as the supreme good. Many see pain as the greatest evil. Seeking pleasure for pleasure's sake is a poor path to guide our lives by. And avoiding pain is not a good thing if we want our relationships to grow which means we may have to process distasteful stuff. No wonder we all despise discipline and pursue pleasure. Many mistake pleasure alone for love. Many mistake pain for something intrinsically evil, and something that should be avoided altogether.

Because we all use these indicators at least partially on the maps we are making or following, we (some more than others) don't always recognize love for what it truly is. Saint

Paul says about those who pursue Love:

> For now we see only a reflection as in a mirror; then
> we shall see face to face. Now I know in part; then I
> shall know fully, even as I am fully known.[46]

I heard a story once of a man who spent a considerable
amount of time trying to understand one of the more difficult
sayings from Saint Paul found in the New Testament. He
spent days looking for the meaning of the saying, but could
not penetrate its mystery. He finally gave up, thinking that
Paul did not want to be understood.

I don't fault the man for giving up, but I do disagree with him
that Paul did not want to be understood by others. Paul said
that he himself would much rather say a few words in an
intelligible tongue, than many in a foreign tongue[47]. The key
to understanding Paul is in walking the path that he did. He
pursued a relationship with God through much hardship,
suffering, faith and action.

Few have exceeded Paul's determination and passion. Some
understanding comes easy and naturally, some understanding
comes through great study, some understanding comes from
suffering for noble causes, some understanding comes from
connecting with people or God. The understanding that
comes out of searching for how to love is by far the most
difficult to acquire as it means we have to confront blockages
to love, and go deeper with God who is deeper still.

---

[46] 1 Corinthians 13:12
[47] Cf. 1 Corinthians 14:19

I'm not saying that we should seek out the exact same suffering and danger that Paul went through for the express purpose of understanding him more completely. That would be madness. Life is far too difficult as it is. And love doesn't seek knowledge or understanding for their own sake. Everything Love seeks has to do with giving life. Yes, in seeking to love we come to many truths; but seeking truth does not usually lead to love or life. There is natural life, and then there is super-natural life. What will we pursue at the expense of the other?

The Means and The Ends Of Love:

> And now these three remain: faith, hope and love. But the greatest of these is love.[48]

Faith and hope are the means to finding love and giving supernatural love. Because only with God's help can we love in a supernatural way; faith and hope put us in relationship with Him so that He can transform our hearts from being hard to being soft and docile to His Spirit. Faith and hope are only important to the degree that they enable us to love.

Love? Why do it? It will cost us. It's up to us if we want to patiently pursue its conception, birth, and growth, maturity, and consummation with God's help.

---

[48] 1 Corinthians 13:13

9 HOW TO MOTIVATE LOVE

So, how does one cultivate doing acts of love? Some people think that in order to love one has to feel like doing it. Others think that no emotion is needed, and that love is only a decision, or a duty.

How one views what love is can either enrich our actions or make them very stale or make them non-existent. It can either increase our harvest of love or diminishes it.

If love is only a feeling then we will emphasize those feelings more than doing something real and substantial for others. After all, love does involve actions.

On the other hand, if love is only a decision then we will only do rigid mechanical actions. We will lack warmth and affection towards those we think we are loving. And so those receiving our version of love may not accept our actions as being real love.

If we have no emotions or feelings for those we claim to love, then we will in all likelihood not have heartfelt love for them. But having affection for others does not guarantee that we will love them either. The ideal is to be able to have warm emotions that help motivate us to love, but this is not often the case.

The Gospels say that Jesus had compassion for those He loved. Many people don't feel compassion and I didn't for a long time either. Many say they won't wait around to feel compassion in order to love because then, they will never love. I have learned that if we are in the habit of being full of self-pity when requests are made of us, and/ or we use angry pressure to get our way, then we will never have real or substantial compassion for others.[49]

To have compassion means to both share in another's sufferings and to work towards relieving it in ethical ways. People, who don't feel compassion for those suffering, when they should, either are numb inside (have shut down inside because they got stuck processing stuff from the past), are wounded, or they actually have insensitive or hard hearts. It is true that we don't need to have feelings to love others a lot of the time, but if we lack compassion (which involves feelings) then we are missing out. I don't want to miss out on love, do you?

There are two exceptions. Namely, when health-care professionals have to see people with injuries, diseases, or illnesses all of the time, then it can be difficult for them to feel compassion all the time if they have no place to lay down their burdens: they too need a way of processing such burdens of negativity. Those who partake in wars can see so much destruction that they get used to it, or they break down inside getting stuck and unable to process all that belongs to how wars are fought. Mankind was not designed to be absorbed with such suffering. We were designed to feel joy and happiness day in and day out. Insensitivity or lack of

---

[49] Cf. My book called, Dismantling the Tree of Knowledge of Good and Evil Within So Love Can Thrive that shows how to jettison self-pity and angry pressure, and win through to compassion.

compassion are rooted in pride and are kept alive by using angry pressure and self-pity to get one's way. But one also needs to deal with the pride, fear, and hurts in the different contexts of our relational lives as these block love too.

Procrastination, and sloth are killers of love. So is not wanting to pay the cost of doing acts of love. So what is the remedy, if any? Renewing the heart and mind in the context of a love relationship with God. Finding a spouse will help too, that is, if we work on our own "shit" and refrain from obsessively demanding correct behavior from our spouses or trying to correct our spouses.

We will partially love other people the way we see God loving them; and also by how we love ourselves. If we have felt God's love and touch, then we will want to love others in the same way. But getting there can be elusive if we lack wisdom. We get wisdom through reasoning with God in our thoughts (known as two-way prayer) and (two-way Journaling) with the back drop of Scripture, and a confessor or other believers.

How we speak to ourselves is often the way we believe God speaks to us too. The devil is harsh, mean, tries to force things, puts pressure on us, threatens us, and uses false guilt, shame, and fear to get us to do stuff. If we see God like this in some ways, then we are confused and won't have much love in our lives. God, rather, is gentle, real, kind, sober, caring, and appeals to our nobleness, to our desires to love, and our caring. God's voice is authoritative and rings like truth, so it sets us free; but the devil's voice is deceptive and leads away from Relationship with Jesus and into slavery.

We won't always feel God's love. So, we will need to believe in it when it seems absent. We need to thirst for love to love; thirst is a foundation stone to love. Thirst is like commitment. It helps us love when things get difficult. We have a supernatural love tank, and when it is empty we can't supernaturally love; only God can fill it if we allow Him to as we continue to seek and embrace practicing humility; God wants to fill it. When we aren't feeling God's love we should believe in it anyways. Believing in God's love is foundational to loving others supernaturally. His love should lead to humility in us. Humility brings grace and freedom. Real humility brings caring; and caring finds a way to love and eventually enables us to feel compassion for people.

It is unhealthy to be dry spiritually inside unless it is part of a journey that God is leading us through as He seeks to bring us into the Promised Land.

If we are wounded, we will likely wound others. If we love ourselves healthily we will more likely love others in healthy ways too. We have consciences and beliefs. When they contradict each other then we know we have business to attend to. We must process our feelings and beliefs in healthy ways through honest, deep, connecting prayer where we reason with God about what is happening inside of us without pushing the negative down. There are ways to processing unhealthy thinking, beliefs, attitudes, and sin strongholds; and ways of growing in the virtues.[50]

---

[50] Cf. My book called, Dismantling the Tree of Knowledge of Good and Evil Within so Love Can Thrive

How we think also determines the quality of our love for others. Often old lie-based-codes written on our minds and hearts take time to be removed and replaced with healthier ones. The reason those codes are there is because we trusted each of their sources, or there was just enough truth in the lies to win us over; or our judgments, anger and search for revenge, or our commitment to not be hurt again kept us from seeking restorative justice or blinded us to reality.

Getting in touch with that part in our hearts that cares for people, in touch with our gratitude; and practicing mindful genuine thanksgiving for the forgiveness of our sins brings peace, joy and level-headedness that enables God to cleanse us from unhealthy self-pity and anger. When we have gratitude, we will be less tempted by greed, we won't be as envious or selfish and so we will want to share with others what we have been given: mercy, grace and love; and God's presence.

In my journey, when I had grown a bit more humility, and I thought about praying to God: "Please tell me whatever you want me to do, and I will do it." I would feel fear and get scared of what God might actually ask me to do. My thinking was that if God wants me to do something I don't want to do, and He asks me to do it, then I will have plenty of guilt to deal with. I know that there are things that I definitely would not want to do. So, I have learned to not ask the above when not fully committed.

God has no joy in making us feel guilty. I also learned that it is easier to pray to God saying, "Please make me an instrument of your peace [today, O God]."[51] That way I am more likely to do God's will without worrying about the prospects of feeling guilt and failure knowing I did not want to do something He asked me to do. I realized that I would most likely do God's will (by praying as suggested) even when I land up being oblivious to the fact that I'm actually doing God's will. That's why I pray The Lord's Prayer because in it I say to God: "your will be done."

On the other extreme, when I was a babe in Christ I used to pray: "God please tell me what to do" believing I would do it without doubt or hesitation. But now that this pride and confidence has been challenged enough for me to know I'm not always up to it, I'm not so naïve anymore.

If I go to God half committed to doing His will on an issue I will have a 50% chance of coming away with guilt. Thankfully there is forgiveness, but why waste God's time? Don't ask God if you are not committed to full obedience in the area you are focused on.

Seeing the cost of each act of love should not necessarily make us shrink back. We don't have to dread counting the cost. We don't have to suppress the cost to conquer the cost of loving others. What makes caring so special is that it overcomes obstacles including those barriers in our minds and hearts to loving people. Love attempts to focus on the pros and handles the cons or negatives in each situation that it encounters with positivity. Love doesn't set its heart on each thing going its way. Whether it is the flesh or just human

---

[51] Inspired by Saint Francis of Assisi

nature that opposes doing unselfish acts, the only way to overcome them for a Christian is to abide in Jesus the True Vine through a humble faith in a teachable fashion and to become dependent on Jesus.

To love we have to accept each person for where she or he is at and not where we expect or want her or him to be. We do this by humbling ourselves. When we care for people, and when we accept where they are at without judgment, that is when we can become gracious towards them.

Love does not measure (i.e. judge) people and despise them. Love doesn't manipulate, put angry pressure on, twist, control, and demand that others change. Love doesn't scream unfairness, trying in a self-pitying dark negative way to get what we want from people. Love does not force or threaten change. When we start to accept others where they are at we will get in touch with where we are at. That is where and when we can start to renew our minds with God's help and so advance in love. When we accept others where they are at we will get in touch with what is in our hearts. We will also begin to see and accept what is in our hearts and minds. Love does not push down and try to keep the bad from coming out of our hearts. Love healthily processes our bad energy, emotions, thinking, beliefs, and attitudes until they are replaced with their respective virtues. We don't have to be afraid of the bad within us, just respect its presence, and if it is a compulsion then God can free us from it.[52]

---

[52] Cf. My book called, Dismantling the Tree of Knowledge of Good and Evil Within so Love Can Thrive.

Principles and theories and rules are all fine and well, but they are not enough all by themselves. We don't need algorithms more than warm healthy relationships. We need both grace filled relationships and truths, and Jesus provides both.

Saint Augustine taught that the love between God the Father and God the Son was so rich, powerful, pure and righteous that it was the third person of the Holy Trinity: God the Holy Spirit. So, if the love between the trinity is the Holy Spirit, ought it not be the same between and for us mere human beings?

Anyone who wants to supernaturally love must not neglect the Holy Spirit: the third person of the Holy Trinity that is if they know about Him. He who welcomes the Holy Spirit welcomes supernatural love. Jesus is the True Vine, and what flows through His branches into those persons who abide in Him is not just only life giving power. Rather it is the Holy Spirit; that inexhaustible source of goodness, insight, and love. He is ever gentle, peaceful, full of good counsel, and generous with His grace. He is also an approachable person, ever present, and joyfully alive who guides us into bearing the good fruit promised to those who seek to love Jesus' way. The good fruit being love, joy, peace, patience, gentleness, goodness, faithfulness, meekness, and self-control.[53]

There are no formulas, algorithms or recipes or sets of rules that we can implement to force or obligate the Holy Spirit to make us supernatural lovers. God owes us nothing. The path

---

[53] Galatians 5:22

to God's heart is humility, teachableness, seeking healthy attitudes, not judging Him, and not accusing Him. He comes and goes where He pleases. He wants into our lives, and "The Prayer to the Holy Spirit" by Cardinal Mercier can be a healthy beginning each and every day. It is easily found with a Google search.

Praying it in faith He will answer it. By faith I mean not only believing that it is possible, but that you will love, and grow in love towards others in the present. Why? Because Jesus said that, "Everything is possible for those who have faith"[54] and Saint Paul said that, "We can do all things through Christ Jesus who strengthens us."[55] Believing that God will help us to love and grow in love by virtue of our faith in Him and being teachable is a reality to all who embrace these truths. Our faith turns: "I can do all things through Christ Jesus who strengthens me" into: "I can love all who come my way through Christ Jesus who strengthens me."

Jesus will slowly remove obstacles, baggage, dirt, and lies that have kept our loves for people shallow or weak. Listening to Jesus' voice and not jumping ahead of Him thinking we know where He is going is key to growth. We repent in response to Jesus' call; we don't repent so that we can hear Jesus' voice. Jesus' voice is not only heard in our consciences when we sin, but in a multitude of positive ways too. It is God's kindness that leads us to repentance.

Truth that comes from God is intended to make us strong in

---

[54] Mark 9:23
[55] Philippians 4:13

our identity, self-esteem, sense of worth, hope, faith, and love. God's truth is to be used to fight off the lies from the world and the devil. Satan means to use lies to destroy God's image in us and any truthful perceptions of the image of God in our beliefs.

Nothing is impossible for her or him who has faith. It is our faith that overcomes the world. Faith in a good and loving God!

Where is the power to love people supernaturally going to come from? By embracing the grace of the Lord Jesus Christ through faith and jettisoning one's trust in the Law and oneself to bring about good works, right behavior, and salvation. Jesus wants to lead us, He wants to teach us, He wants us to bear much good fruit, and He wants to save us from sin. The law makes nothing perfect[56], it only points out sin[57]. Grace is not a license to sin. The power of sin is in the law.[58] Either embrace Jesus or embrace the law. The former will lead to love, good works and good fruit, whereas the latter will lead to judging, anger, self-pity, bitterness, depression, legalism, bad assumptions, condemnation, judging, anxiety, hatred, malice, and criticism.

The New Testament is about bearing good fruit. The Old Testament LAW-mentality is about rule keeping. There is power in the Good News of Jesus Christ. Being rule based leads to negativity and unhealthy relationships because the

---

[56] Hebrews 7:19
[57] Romans 3:20
[58] 1 Corinthians 15:56

rules eventually become more important than people. Rules can take away our focus on caring for people, and this leads to disconnection.

Healthy use of healthy rules is healthy.

The Law when we put our hope or expectation in it to get us to obey it engenders: I got to, I have to, I must, and I need to or else I'll go to Hell. It dries up love, gentleness, peace, hope, and makes us miserable; whereas grace through faith in Jesus as the source to love brings warmth into our lives, His peace, new desires to love, and good fruits. It also puts within us a desire to not sin. As a person thinks or believes in her or his heart so they will be. So if we want to change our behaviors then we need to change how we think in our hearts. This involves confession to God, repenting in prayer, renewing the mind, becoming dependent on God, and submitting to God.[59]

Those who are caught between the law and grace will do well to rest in the Good News writings from Saint Paul found in the New Testament. And also to peer into the life of the person known as Jesus Christ through the Gospels. God's word is utterly trustworthy: Like Saint Augustine said: The New Testament is revealed in the Old, and the Old Testament is explained in the New. Embrace God's word in the New Testament and a rich harvest will come to you as you listen to and obey the Holy Spirit. Ignore it and your barns will be empty. Don't put your trust in rigid rules, put it in the person of Jesus Christ. He will guide you into love, life, commitment,

---

[59] Cf. My book called, Dismantling the Tree of Knowledge of Good and Evil Within So Love Can Thrive

hope, and peace.

The Old Testament Law was about creating a fair, and respectful society, but all too often the people who tried to adhere to it landed up caring more about what is fair for themselves and not about what is fair for others. Instead of protecting the rights of others, Law observers too often seek to protect their own rights. Now the fairness aimed at in the OT Law was with good motive, but it was a minimum standard, that by itself gave no one power to keep it. The NT Teachings and commands aim higher than the minimal standard given in the OT Law. In aiming for the higher commandments given by Jesus, the minimum standard is fulfilled. This is only done through grace and connection with Jesus through trust in Him.

The only place that the Law has in a Christian's life is to point out sin. We are not under Law, but grace.

God is love. That means that He loves absolutely everyone unconditionally (without conditions). We don't have to change for Him to love us. He loves us so that we can and will change with His help. His love is new every morning. We don't have to be good or perfect for God to love us. When we sin no matter how grievously God does not love us any less. We are all stamped with God's image. We are all made for Him. He has not destined anyone to Hell. He does not threaten anyone. Hell is where we miss out on bearing the full image of God as far as love is concerned within us, if we land up there. God loves us because He is love. What we believe about the image of God's character in our minds and hearts will determine how we love, if (that) at all. If our feelings and attitudes run against our consciences, then we have work to do in prayer; we need to constantly go deeper because God is still deeper.

There is nothing more powerful that motivates love than God's love. His wrath is giving us what we want. If we try to use fear of punishment to grow our love, we will be disappointed. If we try to use "I have to" in order to love, we will be disappointed.

The foul rubbish that is being washed out of our hearts, as our minds are being renewed is only possible with healthy focus points: the goodness of the holy Trinity as revealed in the Scriptures. If we get full of self-pity, and anger; and start judging or attacking God we won't inherit the lavish promises from God until we repent.

When we seek for truth we won't necessarily find love, we often find pride. If we care enough for people, we will find ways (wisdom, truth, grace, and Jesus) to help us to love people. Like Pope Francis said, we must love people more than concepts.

Once we start loving people in supernatural ways we will want to grow in worshipping God by giving Him the glory He deserves, the side benefit being that our pride does not make our love rot, decay, and waste away. God deserves our worship if we don't think He does then we likely think we deserve the glory He has. God does not need our worship; we need to worship Him for our own good. He is the only being that deserves our worship. And our worship of Him won't go to His head. We don't worship God out of fear like those who worship Idols. We worship God out of thankfulness, joy, and peace. Love is not that we have loved but that God has first loved us.

10 ABIDING IN JESUS

One of my most favorite passages in Scripture has been John 15 where Jesus calls Himself the true Vine. Initially I found it compelling, and beautiful; but there were parts that confused me, and I really did not have a good grasp on how to abide in Jesus. I knew that faith was necessary. But I was confused about how good works figured into the equation.

Then when I first started working again (not volunteering) after I got schizophrenia, my back was injured and I had spasms of pain shooting down one of my legs. Thanks to my friend Anita I saw a Massage-Therapist and he not only healed my injury but he said something that cleared up my confusion. He said, "We abide in the Vine to bear good fruit; we don't bear fruit in order to abide in the Vine." That hit my truth center with real forceful conviction.

I have known that we walk by faith not sight especially in the darkness. That means our circumstances can be rough but it is our faith that gets us through. It also means that interiorly when we don't sense the Lord's presence we walk by faith because He promises to never leave nor forsake us. Let's not live for feelings: more pointedly let's not live for pleasure alone.

An undying loyalty to, a commitment to Jesus for who He really is keeps us abiding in the true Vine. When the enemy pursues us, barrages us with fiery darts, lies to us in the contexts of unfairness, slimes us with temptations, and tries to shame us with guilt or reminds us of disappointments then commitment to Jesus is very important. The devil tries to condemn us when we sin seriously; therefore, knowing that God forgives us is crucial to abiding in the Vine. Commitment to our faith in Jesus gets us to stand up each time we fall down.

Some people think that turning away from sin comes before forgiveness. This is not true. Often we are caught in sins that we have no idea on how to get out of. We don't pull ourselves up by our own boot straps to get Jesus to love us! When we confess our sins to God, we should be aware that we may fall into our sins again very soon. In fact we might not even have a proven strategy to prevent us from sinning again in certain areas. We might not know how to stop the sins we do in this life. But if we are sorry for them, we need to speak it out to God in prayer, opening up our consciousness to God. Confession lets God's forgiveness into our lives, and the peace we receive from the Holy Spirit within through forgiveness, gives us hope, and bolsters our trust that all things are possible with God including being washed clean from our sins.

I have searched for years on how to overcome my barriers to love, or put another way: how to repent. Each person must search for how they are to motivate themselves to loving people. I have had a lot of people give me good advice but if I had no humility (I'm still not completely humble) I would have tossed their words behind me and been poorer for it.

Humility is a gift from God for those who ask for it and don't let time, hardship, seeming unfairness, self-pity, pride, injustices, anger and lack of progress separate them from this quest. Searching for true humility centers us in Jesus. Humility isn't a goal in itself, but it is a means to love. Humility is not the focus, love is.

God's love and forgiveness are what attracts us to Him. That connection whether we have it, or whether we are searching for it again through confusion, doubt or fog, compels us forward and steadies us in our walk with Jesus: Him abiding in us and us in Him.

In order to love, if this is what one decides one wants to do. One needs to not put angry pressure on oneself. God does not lead or drive us via a whip as if we were slaves. Neither should we drive ourselves with whips (which is very easy to do...and to be blind to doing). If we want to love then we need to abide in the true Vine – Jesus, and at the same time search for ways to overcome our barriers to love (this is true waiting).[60]

One needs patience and humility to accept where we are at and not to get proud because of what we have done, and not to get discouraged about what still needs to be learned, grown, or be achieved. If one wants to love one will forever consider oneself to be a student of LOVE... to not have mastered love and moved onto other "so called" more important things. Therefore, killing strongholds of pride and replacing them with humility is so important.[61]

Prayer is pivotal to growing in love. The book by Brad Jersak: *Can You Hear Me?* and those by Mark Virkler on journaling prayer give good foundations on two-way prayer and how we can be certain about whose thoughts are who's in our heads, when in conversation with God.

---

[60] Cf. John 15

[61] Cf. My book, Dismantling The tree of knowledge of good and evil Within So Love Can Thrive is so useful to get a handle on how pride corrupts us and how to win the battles against it.

One needs gentleness and the realization that God is the reason for love in our lives and not so much a bunch of principles. If God is the reason for the supernatural love in our hearts then praising, giving glory to, and worshiping Him without end will keep the love we act out from spoiling through our pride.

A shallow prayer life will not sustain a strong love life. Love is humble: it is always learning, it is always a student, it is always a servant/ leader, and it has never arrived. Just like U2's 2009 CD title says: "No Line On The Horizon." There is no finish line in this life until we die. Love does not look down on others who are only now asking the questions we used to ask.

Showing what one perceives to be one's riches in order to entice God to use us never works. Showing God one's poverty does get Him to show His compassion, (restorative) justice, grace, and mercy. Real prayer does not try to impress God. God is no respecter of persons (i.e. He loves you no less or no more whether you are a janitor, a lawyer, or a politician). Love flows from God. Love is God's idea. We don't impress Him so He will include us. All we can do is respond to His call with willing hearts.

Birthing love is painful. It requires faith and endurance. Even though love is God's idea, He has put that desire to love in our hearts at the moment of conception in our mothers' wombs. God gives this desire to us because its end is to bring us true fulfillment. It is an act of kindness on God's part. This all means that even before we met, meet or get to know

Jesus we have the desire to love in our hearts and this is a preparation for the Good News of Jesus Christ.

There are times in the course of our relationships, where people might reveal stuff to us that we have judged in the past up to the present as unacceptable to such a degree that we would be tempted and motivated to push them away from us and never have anything to do with them again. It is OK to feel this way because that means we are at a crossroads, and God is calling us to give up these judgments. If we choose to love them despite the revelations we will grow in love. It is meant as an opportunity for growth, and not meant to be seen as a humiliating failure.

12 BEING GOOD TOWARDS OTHERS, OR LOVING OTHERS

Being outwardly good towards others is not necessarily the same as loving others in each case. It is true that when one loves, one is being inwardly and outwardly good. But being outwardly good alone to someone doesn't always mean that we have loved that someone. If we think that the good that we do somehow earns us a place in Heaven, then we have not loved those we did good towards. And in this case we might very likely be aiming for the path to Hell. Heaven is granted through the forgiveness of one's sins.[62] Love does not ask for wages in return, because it seeks to give sacrificially, without any strings attached to it, and it is also motivated out of thankfulness for what God has given. Love is God's idea, not ours!

If love could earn us a place in Heaven, then we would have something to boast about. But love doesn't boast about one's achievements, rather it gives glory to God, the true and only source of life and authentic love. Every time we boast about a good act in an effort to seek glory for ourselves, the act can't be regarded as love anymore. Love always brings God glory.

God does not need our worship. He deserves our worship. We need to worship Him. Why? Because when we refuse to worship God, then we get proud and arrogant. And that pride leads away from authentic natural and supernatural loves and leads to judging, anger, hatred, hurt, self-pity, and death. I

---

[62] Cf. Luke 1:77

need to and want to worship God more and more because I have enough pride to keep me busy[63].

Love Is Not Motivated By Fear Of Punishment:[64]

When one is trying to avoid sin because one fears being punished by God if one were to sin, then this obedience has nothing to do with love. Fact is: "sin kills us; not God." When we sin we push God away a little or a lot, God does not withdraw from us when we sin; we push Him away when we sin. God is life; so, when we push Him away it brings death to us in little or BIG ways. But faith in and acceptance of God and His ways can bring His grace into our lives to counter our sin, heal us, give us life, hope and a future.

God did not punish Jesus on the cross for our sins; and neither will He punish us for our sins; sin is its own punishment; our sins kill us; God does not kill us. Sin kills us, sin's nature is to hurt, destroy, bring death and to remove the image of God from how we are designed. The devil comes to kill, steal and destroy; not God. God is not in cahoots with the devil. By "cahoots" I mean that the devil would do his best to deceive and kill people and then hand them over to God for Him to punish and put them to death. God does not come to condemn but to save, heal, and give life to all. Jesus came to undo the works of the devil. Fear of punishment from an angry God as an attempt to motivate love won't work because fear and punishment would be the focus, not love.

---

[63] For more on the topic of humility see my book: Exploring Humility and Pride.

[64] I am in debt to Brad Jersak for inspiring the content for this section.

Moving from fear and punishment to caring, compassion, and concern for others is what motivates love. Seeing sin as hurtful towards people and ourselves is more powerful at stopping it than having a fear of God giving us punishments.

Fear of Hell is healthy, we have to keep our destination in mind as we navigate through this life as it reminds us of the consequences of our sins; except for God's grace.

Trying to motivate love by fear of punishment by an angry god is Law-focused and it just can't work. The Law makes nothing perfect. Perfect love casts out all fear. Perfect love does not motivate us by fear. God does not come by and say: "I see you have sinned... so as your punishment I am going to kill you"; neither does He say, "if you sin I am going to punish you with death". Rather, the sting of death is "sin" not "God":

> "Where, O death, is your victory? Where, O death, is your sting?" The sting of death is sin, and the power of sin is the law. But thanks be to God! He gives us the victory through our Lord Jesus Christ.[65]

There is something in sin that kills us. If we believe that people ought to be punished by God on top of the consequences of their sins after they die; except for grace. Then in this life we will think all sins need to be punished to somehow prevent it, especially when it comes to those who provoke us. This can make us very judgmental, mean, and hateful towards each other. And, the focus becomes keeping out of trouble and not necessarily loving people. Said

---

[65] 1 Corinthians 15:55- ??57

differently, people become more focused on: not sinning, instead of doing acts of love. This is not healthy because people focus more on what they aren't doing than on practically caring for people out of love. The best defense is a healthy offense.

> For the wages of sin is death, but the gift of God is eternal life in Christ Jesus our Lord.[66]

Jesus came to save us from sin and death; not to reward us with death as punishment for sin. Jesus does not pay out the wages of sin. He hates sin and death. He came to conquer sin and death. They are His enemies! God is not in cahoots or partnership with the devil.

God does not condemn anyone, or try to manipulate or coerce us (force or threaten us) to love Him or to choose the life He offers. Those who reject God condemn themselves because they cut themselves off from the fount of Life; this Life is God. God has set boundaries and warns us to choose life not death. Death is losing the image of God that we are created in. His image is a precious gift, that the devils try to steal. God does not participate in the devil's schemes, or try to finish those same schemes the way the devil desires.

If we see actions in terms of rules to be kept we will be quick to judge and get angry with others for non compliance. Whereas, if we have desires for other people's actions to be a certain way, then we are sure to be disappointed when they come up short. Healthy disappointment is healthier than

---

[66] Romans 6:23

judging people.

I now know that sin kills us, not God. God does not punish us with death when we sin. When we sin we pull away from life either a bit or a lot: that life is God. Knowing that Jesus did not save us from His Father's wrath, but that the trinity comes to find all who are lost, heal all who are sick, and bring life where there is death; gives me a new desire to stay away from compulsively judging others.

Abiding in Jesus the True Vine does help me to stay away from sinning. This insight that "sin kills us; God does not..." thanks to one of Brad Jersak's books: *A More Christ Like God*, helps me view God more realistically. I no longer fear God's wrath like before, and it also helps me to abide in the True Vine: Jesus, and to fellowship with God. I also have a new appreciation of wanting to stay away from my sin because of its consequences. Now that I see God in this new light I also want to imitate Him, and I don't feel the compulsion to be overly angry and abrasive with others as much as before because of sin.

Moreover, I no longer focus on the possibility of punishment as the only deterrent to not sinning. Seeing sin and its awful consequences is more of a deterrent than fear of the popular understanding of Hell where a God supposedly delights in punishing those there. The former appeals to caring for humanity; the latter is purely self-preservation. When one starts to care more about others "in the now," instead of whether one is going to hell or not, then a healthier love is forged. With this paradigm: "Sin kills us; not God" one slowly moves towards having unhealthy fear cast out of oneself because God no longer appears to be the enforcer, policeman, jailor, and torturer; but He is LOVE itself. The devil is the one that comes to steal, kill, and destroy. God gives life: Jesus came to give life. People who are condemned condemn themselves. God only reaches out to them in kindness; God does not condemn. Like Brad Jersak writes:

> Wrath... is a metaphor for the intrinsic consequences of our refusal to live in the mercies of God.[67]

If we think that somebody owes us for a noble deed we did for them, then they will feel like they have to work off a debt and won't feel loved by us. They will feel trapped, maybe even despise us, and feel tempted to abandon us when and where possible. Thinking somebody owes us is a sure way to make enemies and terminate relationships. Love does not demand friendship. Love cares for people, it always sets people free, and does not blackmail anyone. Love does not put a price on a relationship and try to collect.

In a conversation with God excerpt in the first book I ever wrote, it is interesting that God said, "He was digging tunnels of love in me" ...not, "building muscles of love in me" so long ago (in my Dark Night)... the former gives God the glory whereas the latter would have birthed pride in me because I would have focused on how many love muscles I had. I'm like a glove and God is the hand; or God is the Vine and I'm a branch.

---

[67] Brad Jersak, A More Christlike God

Trying to control others, and argue them into submission is very unhealthy. I have been guilty of this so very often. When we feel we see things, and have wonderful insights it is too easy to get preachy. I know that God has spoken to me many times through people indirectly, but it does not clue into my mind immediately in each situation that what was spoken to me was from God. The Holy Spirit would later convince me that the words spoken applied to me depending on the context. He does not do so to make us feel shame and condemned, but for us to have a change of heart, and to joyously go our way thereafter changed. Correcting people when we have plenty to correct in ourselves (think our consciences) is hypocritical, unloving, and should be abandoned. Thankfully God loves us so much that He does all in His power to convince us to not go down the path of judging people.

When we pray, "God, please help 'so and so' be more like "ME" in this area of love or humility" we are being proud and judgmental. We ought not compare and put others down and attempt to raise ourselves up in prayer or out of it. When we do grow in love and humility we will give glory to God and grow in gratitude. Let's not pretend that we are paragons of virtue. We all have gaps in our thinking, reasoning, understanding, philosophies, and we all fall short in our actions to love and be completely humble. All of us to some degree major on minor issues, and we all minor on many major issues.

PART II

13 EXPLORING HOPE

Hope had long been a virtue that was hard to get my mind, heart, and will around. The following is what God has shown me and has had lasting influence in my daily walk with Jesus. Hope is connected to both faith and love and helps us practice both!

> Hope is what gives faith substance! Faith in part is being sure that what you hope for will come true. Hope gives faith life. Therefore, well-placed hope gives life.

Do not look for hope in your circumstance! No amount of analyzing your circumstances will create hope; because circumstances don't predict the future. Circumstances change with time. But circumstances do help shape us and strengthen our hope commitments especially when the circumstances look hopeless and we carry on anyways. No one needs hope if they can see the future. Deciding to go forward with a goal or to quit based on current circumstances means one is not navigating the situation with hope. Deciding to go forward in a relationship despite having rocky or awkward interactions means one is navigating with hope. Hope believes things can change for the better. If one has hope one has faith! Faith is what overcomes the world, and life's obstacles.[68]

There are different kinds of hope! Hoping that the weather will be sunny here in Vancouver is often wishful thinking! But planting a crop in a field requires more than wishful-thinking-hope. This is because full or empty bellies might be at stake. The future is at stake. Both loss and gain are possible: hope involves risk.

Lighthearted confidence is not hope! Confidence comes from repetition that leads to mastering skills in the present. Lighthearted confidence has to do with the "present" or where situations are controlled or known; whereas hope has to do with the "future" and the unknown; those places that are unfamiliar. Lighthearted confidence here does not get us far into the future when trials and darkness enter into the picture. Hope can. Hope does.

Superstition is an enemy of both hope and faith. It is also an enemy of confidence. We all know of professional sportsmen who base their careers on the foundation of eating at the same restaurant, or having a good luck charm, or having certain rituals, or not going to certain parts of town before the BIG game. These players have superstitions because the real reason for their success is hard work, training, and perfecting skill sets with the help of trainers. Being able to look into the past to not always see success but to see oneself improving, getting up after each failure and trying harder can give one hope or confidence in one's skill set so one can overcome the challenges and adversity in the games one

---

[68] Cf. 1 John 5:4

plays.

People who don't practice hope and also don't have some sort of faith are often very needy and insecure in relationships. This is because they seek for hope in their circumstances that happen to change all the time or they seek it in people whose moods fluctuate or who have other priorities or aren't the nurturing kind! True hope is anchored in a love that is constant, enduring, usually from a mother or father figure or significant other; but mostly from God! Love displaces fear and helps us to hope.

Trust, healthy thinking, and a healthy way of dealing with guilt when we fall short are keys to boosting hope levels! These allow people to know where they stand no matter what the circumstances or intrigues thrown their way! Good leaders can inspire hope! They are able to establish healthy relationships, and that is pivotal for getting hope in their followers to endure the journey or tasks when achieving group and personal goals.

People who practice hope are usually more able to love! Because they have a positive energy that pours out of them! They have healthier attitudes! They aren't as tempted to worry about what they don't have or worry about what others have that they don't have! Hopeful people aren't as easily tempted by jealousy or envy or self-pity, because they are secure and content with what they have and are committed to what is promised. Hopeful people are resilient and have their priorities well set. Setbacks don't loom larger and larger through the moments, hours, days, weeks, years, or even decades, so hopeful people don't have pity parties all the time, or become overly discouraged for long! Hope is powerful medicine in overcoming unrealistic perfectionist attitudes that push one to having to have everything one's way immediately! So, hope helps us to be less self-centered. People with hope don't fall as often into the trap of needing to control others out of insecurity! People with hope are easier to get along with because they are positive and don't focus on their burdens but on their opportunities! People who have hope honor others, wish them the best, and often want to help them get to their destinations.

In our lives, there are hierarchies of duties starting with ones we prefer to do, going down to those we wish we could do without! Many of us would love to jettison those duties we could do without! But once we get to jettison the worst duty the next thing we liked least gets the negative focus and often grows to the stature of what we initially disliked the most! So, we come full circle to square one!

This problem exists because we want to feel good and see doing the undesirable duty as standing in the way of feeling good! Fact is, we don't have to feel good all the time and putting off having to feel good until an undesirable task is done is a quality that those people have who major in hope. Hope isn't needed when things are going well; hope gets us through those circumstances that challenge our goals, and hope gets us to our journeys' ends!

Hope enables patience a characteristic of love. Hope helps us stay away from the "me" mentality - or selfishness. So, it results in giving love to people. Hope helps to fight off envy. It helps us stay away from worry and fear; which shows that love or being loved is operative.

How does hope allow us to grow in love? It helps us because it helps us to choose differently in the present compared to what we chose in the past because of expectations that things can be different in good ways. Believing that we don't have to be stuck in ruts forever and the awful feelings that go with those ruts (think ugly mind pathways and heart habits) gives us hope to navigate into new areas of healthy thinking, believing, feeling, and relating that before may have seemed unimaginable.

This is a slow process that comes through a prayer-connection and relationship with God that sets us free from our unhealthy burdens. Healthy prayer and relationships with Jesus are indispensable to getting our hope levels up. Trying to hold onto permanent-life-changing-hope without God is hard work. We can't make up love as we go along. Love is truth based. It requires that light expose things for what they are one thing at a time: that light is a person: Jesus. He exposes lies so they don't seem like truths anymore and replaces them with real truth. Truth helps hope to grow. The only reasons we believe lies is because they look like truths (when we are threatened or have unreasonable fears), or we wrongly trust the messengers that bring us the lies. Truths set people free to love and break with unreasonable fears.

I remember years back going for walks to a field located somewhere in Vancouver, BC to watch little league baseball games. I witnessed a young lad going up to bat and swinging with all his might only to strike out repeatedly. Each time this happened he proceeded to throw a temper tantrum, sulk, and refused to be comforted by his mother only to repeat this approach repeatedly throughout the season.

I remember thinking that that boy wanted to do what the pros do but without recognizing that a learning curve was needed. One that involves training, correction, dedication, and patience as well as the humility to accept the failures along the way.

Today, I realized that I was that little boy, only I wanted to master the Christian life. I asked the Lord yesterday for a word of wisdom and the word "hope" came again powerfully like so many times before. Hope has a way of helping us practice patience which is an attribute of love. God has shown me many times what love looks like and I always felt disappointed when it was withdrawn from me. Now, I know I don't have to feel disappointed when that happens. All good things come gradually and I need to practice hope (expecting the promises from God to come true) by picking up where I am at and to practice the love I am able to give each part of the journey. There is much to learn, and much to exercise in order to get into the zone, and of course I still will make mistakes.

While in the bends on new roads we don't see our new destinations immediately. The destination may have a name, but what its exact traits, details, and mysteries are, are usually hidden from us. We might have a vague general label for the destination but the details materialize, and only ring fully true, or become familiar once we get to the destination. When in the bend on the road we will have doubts, fears, confusion, and insecurities that will try to pull us back to the familiar; the easy way; to give up our journey.

But thirst for less stagnant waters, along with enough courage and the wanting something new or better is what hope uses to draw us around the bend in the road to a new destination, way of life, skill set, masterpiece, paradigm, way of living, attitudes, occupation, usefulness, loving, understanding, or a new knowing. Because in the bend we don't necessarily know much of anything. We only know that we hope for something better. The not knowing much of anything in the bend of the road is a preparation for new wisdom, new insights, and new growth of love, hope and faith.

I see in this story a parable for my life. God taking my hands in His and enabling me to learn to walk confidently, patiently, kindly, compassionately, wisely, and humbly in a gradual learning process which includes making mistakes, having wrong thinking, experiencing pain, and falling down regularly.

What to Do with Hope?

Repeatedly I'd request urgent revelations for my predicaments from God and frantically search them out without resting in Jesus and learning from Him on how to live in the in-betweenness of the prayer request and the gift. Now I know I can put my time of waiting to healthier uses; I can learn to practice and focus in the here and now while waiting in hope for God to put things into play so the desired gifts or revelations come. Believing that God pours grace into our lives, helps us live in the in-betweenness between a promise and its fulfillment. Hope comes when love casts out unreasonable fears that could otherwise strangle our hopes.

When I don't try to apply myself while waiting for a promise to be fulfilled, then the likelihood of me squandering the gift or revelation immediately or soon after receiving it can be very high. This is because I was only living for the release of the revelation and not for something greater. Living with the promise, is fuller, more practical, and wiser when I search for, practice, and grow into the promise.

In prayer, I'm learning to live in the in-betweenness of requests and corresponding answers. I find that this is a key to living a stable, healthy, gentle, humble, peaceable life that keeps me from squandering my freedoms. The power of hope and trust is grace; and seeking to love makes this possible.

This living for God's gift can turn out to be pretty selfish because it becomes what we live for. We can treat people in the same way by sending them material, giving them our revealed truths , and trying to impress them only to get the same back. Real healthy expectations and hopes are not selfish.

Learning to live in the in-between moments is the key to stability, peace, patience, joy, contentment, and accomplishing things that mean special things to the people we meet. Yes, we can be asked by God to do BIG things at opportune times when they come our way... but the rest of life, everyday life is about practicing the little things. Most of life is about getting the little things accomplished... not just being bored waiting around to do great things. Getting good at the little things is where love grows, where purpose grows, where meaning grows, where confidence grows, where practical giving grows, where faith grows, and where the joy grows.

Faith gets us to open up with God. God's love gets us to hope, because perfect love casts out fear. Unreasonable fears weaken hope. Hope is strengthened when we experience real love.

PART III

14 EXPLORING FAITH

No matter what one seeks to achieve in life, one requires faith to see it through. Whether it is learning a new skill, developing one's aptitude's, acquiring wisdom or knowledge, whether it is navigating relationships, or hoping for a catch while fishing, without faith it won't happen. Sometimes people get faith mixed up with knowing people.

What does it mean to know God? Sometimes, "to know something" means to come to a conclusion through a logical argument. Sometimes, it means to see as a fact. In the Old Testament, it was said that a husband and wife "knew" each other when they had sexual intercourse. In other words, they knew each other because they were intimate, connected, or in a relationship with each other, and this is what I believe is the meaning of knowing God. It means to be connected to and in relationship with Him – the very meaning of Eternal life. It's impossible to know Him as a simple fact. If we did it would be putting God into a box. God is more complex, infinite, subtle, rich, and knowledgeable than we imagine and He really can't be put into a box, but we foolishly try or put Him into them.

Where do faith and knowledge meet in our relationships with God? Is it possible to know all His attributes? After all who of us have seen God's spirit, and so can tell what He is like? Even if we saw Him and His actions when He became man we may never have recognized Him for who He is.

Being in relationship with Him now, we experience His touch, grace and love, but are these enough to keep us from disowning Him when He gives us the bread of adversity and the water of affliction? For when we experience such hardships won't some misconstrue Him as being a fraud who isn't coming through on the goodies a good God would always give? This dilemma is known as the fight of faith. If we doubt, how can it be knowledge? Can we trust our eyes? Can we trust our senses or our memories? Ultimately it takes faith in these gifts in order for us to say we know something. And by faith I simply mean a personal trust.

I'm afraid! And I think that it is a good fear. A fear of saying I know something when in fact I only have faith in it. It is easier for me to say I'm certain about something than for me to say I know it. What is more, the area from my life where it counts the most, I used to have the most confusion about it.

It is like this. God has given me irrefutable evidence that He exists. But I can't necessarily prove this to someone else. He has also given me strong evidence that He is good and loving. So much so, that when He gave me the evidence, I had to say that I was peering inside the heart and mind of God. It was like white hot metal... with the qualities of love, morality, and justice somehow within it. This is the evidence that I hold onto in the face of life's difficulties.

This tension between this having faith in and knowledge of

God is always there. When I talk about my knowledge of God's goodness, I mean that I have tasted from that goodness in ways I never dreamt possible until they occurred.

Do we have a God that is capricious or fickle like some people like to think and teach, or is He Love like the Bible teaches? God gave me the following words from my Mom:

> "O child, you have no idea about the depths of God's love."

But at the time when it was said to me I really didn't understand that this statement had a depth I would only get to know later.

That God would someday somehow let me peek inside His heart was unimaginable at the time. I thought that I would always be left to interpret the good times as His favor, and the bad times as His discipline. Instead of interpreting the good times as being a product of chance, and the bad times a result of God's curse. The idea being that the interpretation can go either way depending on one's faith in the goodness of God or the lack thereof.

I suppose what I'm trying to get at is this. Things are either true, untrue, or a messy mixture of the two in their given contexts. Some people who have claimed to know truth for absolute certainty have also committed some of the most heinous crimes imaginable. Once we know the truth it's supposed to set us free to love as Jesus promised. Yet obviously sometimes we are mistaken about what that truth is.

The chief priests along with the leading citizens of Jesus' day thought that they knew what was right and truthful; and arrested Jesus in order to punish and crucify Him for not being loyal to and obeying their take on the Law.

Then again, many people have claimed to not know what truth is, yet have landed up doing just as much harm. Pilate the man who passed the death sentence on Jesus claimed to not know what truth is at Jesus' trial.

Faith is always accompanied with doubt. Sometimes the faith is so strong that the doubt seems to dry up. Other times the faith is so weak that the doubts torment us horribly. Faith has its useful purposes, but most people would agree that there is something called knowledge. Sometimes knowledge, if it is the right kind, can erase the need for faith and so blow away the doubts too. But how do we get to this place of knowledge?

I am convinced that relational knowledge is held within each of our spirits. Each spirit has the ability, when we listen to it, to discern and read the energies, motives, intentions, and characters of the people we meet. This intuition has an uncanny ability to get it right so often, but we can dismiss it so easily. It grows the longer we know someone. It enables us to trust, or warns us to not trust. It stabilizes us, and allows us to feel the peace and goodwill of others. It connects us to people and God through trust and enables us to feel love, know love, and want to return love. Ultimately this spirit-knowledge gives stability and allows us to function more confidently, with certainty, with foundations, and with peace more so than if we were to just go by faith alone.

I believe in absolute truth. But I won't pretend to have it. Mathematics contains what I would call truths. Are they absolute? No, because they are incomplete to us, we do not see all their conclusions or results, their limitations, their strengths, where they sit in the whole fabric of mathematical knowledge, what they don't or can't answer, and what their complete contexts are. To God, they are absolute because He knows every detail, every scope, every weakness, every strength, every application, and every angle. We aren't so knowledgeable and that is a good thing. It can keep us humble when we keep this perspective.

Math is a tool that we all rely on to some degree or other. All mathematicians would say that math is a good thing. Yet, both good and bad has come from mathematical knowledge.

I'm more passionate about God than I am about math these days. Some claim that God doesn't exist. Yet, God has set me free from many sins, much of which I was blind to for a large part of my life. I know that God exists and that He has set me free. I therefore "believe" that God is absolutely good. But I'm too afraid at this juncture to say that I "know" He is completely and absolutely good in the shadows. I agree that we can know that He has some goodness in Him partly from revelations, partly from how we are made, partly from experience, partly from our spirit-intuitions, and partly from logical arguments.

Here is an Argument:

I claim that if God were pure hatred, then He would have no self-love if in the beginning He was all that existed. To see this, suppose that we are starting out with a God who is pure hatred. Before He created anything, He would have to hate something. That something would have to be Himself since initially He would be all that there is.

If God were pure hatred, He could not even love to hate, He would hate to hate. Every moment would be weariness for Him. What a terrible existence. God could not create creatures that had joy or happiness like we do because He would only create those things that are consistent with His character, which would be things that are consistent with hatred. Since humans do love, we can't have a God that is pure hatred.

A God with any measure of self-love will love whatever He does with that same measure of love. This is because one loves what one produces when one loves oneself.[69] The fact that love exists means that pleasure exists. The ultimate end of love is wholesome life (the ultimate end of pleasure is not always love). To the measure that God loves Himself, He will love His creation, because He would want to find pleasure in it.

A selfish God would never create any happy or joyous creatures because He would be jealous of their joy or happiness. A selfish God would want everything for Himself and so could not share His life with His creatures. If He did

[69] I am in debt to my friend Alex Pruss for this insight.

make creatures, He would want their loyalty at all costs. Any rebellious creatures would not be tolerated – He would will them out of existence the moment before they defied Him. A selfish God would want robots, and not creatures with free will, because He could not stand being rejected. Therefore, a selfish God does not exist, because we aren't robots.

A proud God would be just as insecure as a selfish God. He would never create a creature that could be happy when He himself wasn't the attention of that happiness. He would envy them, and since self-love would be part of His identity, He would not want to lose any pleasure because of His creatures' disloyal behavior. Because people exist and experience joy and happiness that they don't glorify God for at different times, God must be humble enough to permit this. This evidence points to a God who loves, and has no defects.

This isn't a watertight argument for why God must be good. It is good as far as it goes, but one still needs to explain why bad things apparently happen to supposedly good people. Peter Kreeft attempts to answer this question in his book entitled: *Making Sense Out of Suffering*.[70] His conclusion is surprising.

A better question to ask is: Why do good things happen to bad people?[71] The logic behind this question comes down to justice. Certainly a just God would oppose evil, wicked, proud, and rebellious people. But He apparently does not do so, at

---

[70] Peter Kreeft, Making Sense Out Of Suffering, Servant Books (1986)

[71] I am in debt to my friend Chris Brion for this question in this context.

least not in ways we can always see in this life.

Christianity teaches that God is both loving and just. A loving God will forgive people their wrongs when they ask for forgiveness, or when they practice mercy because only merciful people understand and desire forgiveness. Brutal people refuse to secure forgiveness. Proud people are given time to repent by God. This happens often; I know it happens with me daily. But if a proud person refuses to believe the Good News and repent then God can't force His grace on them. They have separated themselves from Him, and that means they will very likely suffer the consequences of their sins.

So much for one of the many arguments for why God is good.

For most people the struggle isn't so much about whether or not God is good, but rather it has to do with whether or not God will be good to them.

This is because we aren't God, and since God is distinct from us, He will have different desires, hopes, expectations, and plans for our lives than what we do, either some, or all of the time. And so faith will be needed to navigate the dark times, and faith is also needed to stay pure through the prosperous times. It is so easy to become corrupt.

Crazy Faith:

We will always need faith of some sort because we don't have absolute knowledge like God does.

The kind of faith in God that seems absurd to have in the face of one's circumstances is what I like to call crazy faith. The kind of faith talked about in the book of Hebrews, chapter 11 in the Bible. This kind of faith goes on despite the insurmountable odds that seem to be against it from a human perspective. Despite the unknowing it perseveres. Despite the doubt it continues.

This is the kind of faith that God expects all of us to exert at some time in our lives. Life is not easy, and the circumstances that it throws at us can shake our faith in God to the very core of our soul's foundations, so much so that we might follow through on the idea of abandoning our faith in God completely at times. The fact that most of us don't abandon our faith in God when we are tested is a miracle! Testing will come, sooner or later, with God there urging us on to the finish line. Self-pity is used by the devil to try and pry us away from dependence on God.

To understand faith a little better, let us look at the time[72] when Jesus walked on water towards the disciples who were in a boat rowing against a strong wind. At first when they saw Jesus and thought that He was a ghost, but Jesus quieted their fears by letting them know that it was Him. Peter then asked Jesus to call him out of the boat so that he too could walk on the water with Jesus. Jesus called Peter, and Peter walked on the water for a while until when?

Some say until Peter took his eyes off of Jesus. This is compelling, but that's not where he makes his error. Some say it's when Peter sees the wind and the waves. Again this is compelling, but that's not where he makes his error. Peter,

---

[72] Matthew 14:22-32

like all of us at different times, made the mistake when he relied on his own fallen understanding of what is true. He went from believing that Jesus had power over the waves and wind, to believing that the waves and the wind had more power than Jesus' love and care for him.

When Peter was first walking on the water, he was aware of his success. As the wind continued to blow and the waves did their dance, the faith in his heart switched its allegiance from Jesus to what made more sense to his spiritually impoverished mind. He relied on his own understanding of how things ought to work instead of exercising his frail faith in Jesus. Deep down inside Peter's heart, he trusted his fallen natural instincts or intuition more than Jesus. Even the strongest Christians when tested will come to such crossroads.

Initially, Peter's faith allowed him to accomplish small things, and to travel short distances. Most of us, like Peter, start out believing Jesus for the little things, but when things get a little more difficult we can't seem to go on as easily. As we grow up in our faith, we become able to do more courageous acts with the doubt still present but with less worry. That's why God created life to be so bumpy. It provides us with opportunities for spiritual growth. God wants us to grow our faiths: our ability to open up to God through thick and thin times.

A stagnant mind, one that is bored with God, spiritual things, and wants to move on is often a result of not being able to tune reliably into God's voice. God wants to exercise our faith so that it can grow up into crazy faith. A faith, that when it encounters the need to walk on water, won't allow our limited understanding of the world (including the wind and waves) and the laws that govern them, to oppose our trust in Jesus and His love.

There is nothing wrong with thinking, and that's not what gets us into trouble. What gets us into trouble is our understanding of what the believable premises are in given situations! Should we believe God or our circumstances? Should we believe and see things negatively? Should we believe and think according to the voices of the world, the flesh and the devil; or God? This is what the Holy Spirit is talking about when He speaks:

> Trust in the Lord with all your heart
> and lean not on your own understanding;
> in all your ways acknowledge him,
> and he will make your paths straight.[73]

It is of utmost importance that we trust whole-heartedly in God even when we don't understand what He is doing through the circumstances in our lives. When we do this we have crazy faith in God, and so can claim to know Him. That is to be in a connected relationship with Him.

For a long time, I felt that the saying, "We walk by faith, and not by sight or feelings" to be very distasteful because I did not understand or see the power that the idea has. Darkness does come into each of our lives, faith helps us weather the

---

[73] Proverbs 3:5-6

storms and keeps us from ship wrecking our hope in our journeys with God.

In the past, I used to be at the mercy of my emotions, and get all stressed or fall into despair when things were threatening. Sometimes I would think: "I should not have done this or that", and I'd get apprehensive; thinking, "I might very likely lose my job now" or I'd think "What on earth does 'so and so' think about me now?" Or, I'd have the accuser saying to me, "You really should not have done that Rene, look at you now, you're nothing, you're hoping for far too much, no one cares about you, you have no friends, no one likes you." Notice how all of these ideas are so fear and negativity focused.

But now I know that my spirit-knowledge (and faith) is meant to do away with these unfortunate fiery darts that the devil is responsible for and loves to shoot at me. My spirit, when it chooses to trust God and the honest people in my life, and is tuned into rational, common-sense practical wisdom, then I am kept safely away from entertaining lies that either have little foundation in reality or as far as possibilities are concerned are so small in probability of occurring that a sensible person in her or his right mind would automatically disregard it without fear or hesitancy.

One of the characters in *The Lord of the Rings* Films named Gollum spoke the negative self-talk like I used above in one of his scenes. The potential for Gollum's attitudes, beliefs, and emotions is in all of us; and can kill our faiths if we aren't careful.

I have found that I can believe in the above negativity and get depressed, frustrated, and want to quit. But there is no easy way out. I can trust in God, and not go by what these negative voices and what these associated feelings say. Reality is rarely what our emotions say they are. Emotions often reflect our insecurities. We often discount how much others love us. Especially how much God loves us. Emotions also reflect our desires. If we desire something that we can't have, then we will usually gravitate towards self-pity if we are immature. But the Kingdom of God is upside down. The world says, "Go by your feelings and desires" or, "If it feels good do it." But God says, "Go by my truth, my light, my promises, and my love." When we connect with God and do it His way through faith, we will eventually feel His peace in our bumpy situations where before it seemed impossible to have peace.

I now know that I can choose to believe my feelings or insecurities, or I can believe what my faith and spirit say. I also know that my feelings are determined by what thoughts I have running through my head. Negative thoughts mean negative feelings. Positive thoughts mean positive feelings. When I change my thoughts, my feelings will follow; I don't have to let the devil set the agenda for what I think. When I do he has lots of fun in making me miserable.

While growing up one will rightly or wrongly acquire many beliefs that are either based on fact, on fiction or on a mixture of the two. As these convictions solidify they will bring about certain emotions and attitudes when challenged. After a while one will not look at how these beliefs were formed but only to the emotions and attitudes they form when challenged. By this I mean that we will eventually think certain actions are wrong or right because they trigger guilt, fear, pride, joy, or a sense of justice or injustice within us. If the process that formed our consciences was flawed, then many of the teachings from the Bible will look ridiculous because our emotions say so. This is where faith is necessary if we want to embrace a real relationship with Jesus. Prayer is important, but so is meditation on God's Word with Jesus as the final interpreter of that Word. Basing our beliefs on truth is where it is at and that is where suffering is so crucial.

Suffering allows us to re-examine, refocus, and reassess what is important, true, and to be valued. When we feel threatened by pain we will often see how we have threatened others with our judgments, actions and beliefs because now we are in the same position. Ultimately we will find what we are looking for. The beliefs I now have resemble something of what I started out with in 1989 after my conversion to becoming a follower of Jesus Christ. But they have been challenged, nuanced, and been corrected in a multitude of ways since then. This process won't stop.

Love has been my goal. And I have been sorely mistaken on what I initially thought it took to love on many counts. Even though I prized love, I used to be very proud, angry, and judgmental. But I have made a lot of progress because Jesus is leading me on the path to freedom through relationship with Him.[74]

In a conversation with a dear brother in Christ I began to realize that there are times when God reveals Himself to me so unmistakably that in those moments I know He is God the Almighty, Absolutely Good, full of Love, compassionate, merciful, and grace-full beyond measure. But when the moments pass and fade I realize that I can't prove in my mind that He has these attributes to others or even myself. In between these encounters I realize that I'm certain about God's Goodness, but that I no longer know it in my mind like I used to be able to prove mathematical theorems on paper with pencils or pens. God is the proof, and when He hides Himself I'm left to depend upon my faith in Him. This used to scare or frighten me earlier in my faith Journey, but now I accept it as a part of the journey I'm on.

Because we can't know anything for complete and absolute certainty, or without doubt to some degree unless God were to constantly reveal Himself, we need courage, the important ingredient that gives life to faith. To claim one has been led into the complete truth and that there ought to be no doubt about what is sin or isn't sin is unwise[75]. Claiming to have absolute knowledge is unwise, and can cause psychosis. Honest people admit they have straw, not absolutes neatly

---

[74] Cf. My books called: Going Deeper With The Twelve Steps, and Dismantling the Tree of Knowledge of Good and Evil Within so Love Can Thrive talk about what processes are necessary to make a healthy recovery from spiritual illnesses.
[75] Saint Paul teaches that for what is sin for one person isn't necessarily so for another in certain circumstances.

spun together in rows of words.

A true faith journey with God keeps us from being complacent or too certain about what we know or of being too pleased with ourselves. It keeps us from getting proud if our hearts are open to the truth and we remain teachable. When we get pleased with ourselves in an area we may more than at other times become tempted into becoming proud in that area. That's why God chose humble faith to determine whether one is righteous or not. Only God can afford to know something absolutely without any doubt this side of Heaven continuously. For He is a holy God, and as the Scriptures say, "God is light; and in Him there is no darkness at all."[76] Here, "light" means perfect goodness, or love, and "darkness" means any hint of evil.

It is important to know that faith without love is worthless. 1 Corinthians 13:2 states, "If I have the faith that can move mountains, but have not love, I am nothing." So, faith in God that is humble helps us remain committed to love and caring for others.

---

[76] 1 John 1:5

PART IV

15 PATHWAYS

All earthly relationships involve navigating disputes. And when we learn that we don't have to judge to get our views considered by another person, then the light shines the brighter into our relationships. And we start to respect people in healthier ways, and this brings more joy into all of our lives.

Telling the truth appeals to another person's nobleness, desire for mercy, humanness, warmth, kindness, and caring. It doesn't try to convict, shame, blame, or disrespect any person. It doesn't put people on the defensive, or make them want to hurt us back and want to judge us back. Judging robs a person of self-esteem, self-worth, and respect.

Not speaking judgmental thoughts is very wise, but it is even healthier to not have judgmental thoughts. If we find we are entertaining judgmental thoughts, then exploring how we feel and using honest "I" statements interiorly helps us to gain perspective and pushes away the judging.

By aiming higher than just not wanting to judge people we can develop habits of thinking and speaking highly of others, and acting kindly and positively towards them, making them feel cared for and loved. This should not be a strategy, it should be the outworking of the Holy Spirit.

There is a danger regarding loyalty to concepts that can lead to a default stance of anger, judgment, and possibly hatred towards people before we even meet them. Usually when we love certain concepts we land up hating other concepts that threaten or go against the concepts we are loyal to. If this is the case, then when people profess loyalty to a concept we abhor, then we can very easily land up hating those same people (before we get to know them on a deeper level) if not careful because of our loyalty to some important concept(s). In this case we don't even give the person a chance of getting into a friendship with us.

When we move to giving up on doing this, then we start learning to love people as they are (like God does), and not judge and hate them as a caricature because of a clash in values. Ideas have a lot of power, we have got to be as wise as serpents and innocent as doves in the way we use concepts.

When people know we love them or that we have good will towards them, then they are more willing and able to handle being corrected in healthy ways by us. Correcting and judging aren't the same things.[77] Jesus set out the conditions for when and how to correct someone caught in a sin. It isn't wise to neglect His wisdom or commands.[78]

No one rejoices over judging; but because of truth's nature those who seek love rejoice over truth.[79]

---

[77] I speak about this topic at length in my book named Exploring Humility and Pride
[78] Cf. Matthew 7:1-6
[79] 1 Corinthians 13:6

In me, in judging a person I harden my heart, and make my tongue toxic. But truth can lead to caring, sympathy, empathy, compassion, kindness, change, and mutual respect; it gives the benefit of the doubt, it believes the best about people[80]. Judging often communicates: "I know better than you, so listen to me!"

The reason why we are very sorely tempted into thinking judgmental thoughts and to want to follow through on judging people is because we feel injustices have been visited on us. Even when we recognize that Jesus commanded us to not judge, we are pulled this way to try to make things right because we think that if we don't speak up things will get worse.

This tension occurs because we don't know how to speak our truth gently. Judging attacks whereas speaking the truth does not. Truth speaking involves using "I" statements and owning our feelings in conversation with those who hurt us and is more likely to illicit understanding and change (although those who don't care may laugh us off) whereas, when we judge, then we blame and put people on the defensive. There will be no healing unless there is forgiveness on both sides.

Years ago, I was promised an opportunity that was not coming through for me. I was tempted to get bitter, hostile, and I had many judgmental thoughts towards the person I thought was responsible for reneging on his promise. But when it came time to confront the person I did not blame him, I said how I felt, I did not vent, hate, scream injustice, or

---

[80] 1 Corinthians 13:7

judge the person. A few days later the opportunity came my way. I now know the person did not feel judged by me, and he was warmed by my response to his cold shoulder. I see this as a powerful example of the difference between judging and telling the truth.

Remembering the many consequences of judging along with what judging is and what truth telling are will help one to stay away from judging. The more we focus on truth telling, and deal with our envy, Pride, fear, and broken relationships in healthy ways the less we will judge or talk behind a person's back.

This diagram below maps some possible paths taken when dealing with human conflicts:

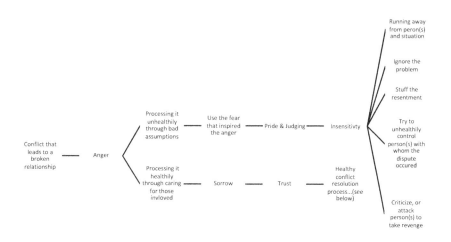

This diagram shows unhealthy and healthy pathways to

dealing with conflicts. When (a) relationships are broken because of conflicts (with long histories or not), they will cause anger because anger alerts us to the fact that stuff is wrong. Anger is neither right nor wrong in this context. It is what it is. It is what we do with anger that can be harmful. If we take the fleshly route, anger is used in an unhealthy way and causes a lot of hurt (human anger does not achieve the righteousness of God).

When we healthily process our anger, then we stay away from sin (hurting people) in the process, and if we do sin in the process (because we aren't perfect) then we will be motivated to deal with it healthily ASAP if we know how.

The Unhealthily Processed Anger:

When we are humanly angry because of a violation, injustice, hurt, or supposed disloyalty, then we can make bad assumptions, and this can make our fears grow that the violation will reoccur, or that the injustice will be perpetually visited on us. This can cause fear and an urgency to do something about it. But because we see the injustice and feel hurt, we can judge the agent of our hurt as worthy of our resentment (and see them as an enemy and harden our hearts towards them). This is all done out of hurt, fear and pride because it says "I need to protect myself at all costs" and "I'm better than them." This leads to insensitivity and a lack of respect for the person. From this, five scenarios can arise:

Scenario (I): Running away. This is often the cowardly or rebellious thing to do which is also a result of being fear driven. Hagar in Genesis 16:1-15 after getting into a dispute with her mistress felt powerless and a lot of self-pity and tried to solve her problems by running away.

Scenario (II): Ignoring the problem. This was Abraham's solution to the mess with Hagar he and his wife had created (Cf. Genesis 16:1-15). It says: it is not my responsibility; you deal with it the way you see fit. I wash my hands of it.

Scenario (III): Stuffing the resentment. This is what I was in the habit of doing in so many of my conflicts. It has the power to kill happiness, love, life, and joy. It creates baggage or jadedness. It has the power to get us seeking after idols to bring happy moments (but idols always bring fleeting moments of happiness). Idols will come our way if this is not dealt with healthily. The resentment need not always be against the person(s) you have had the conflict with, it can be directed to yourself for having gotten yourself into the situation in the first place and for the things you did in the situation that you are not proud of.

Scenario (IV): Attempting to control the person(s) to get our happiness back (but we can't change anyone). Attempting to control may mean any one of many strategies is adopted. Using force, threats possibly, using angry pressure, meanness, impatience, inappropriate boundary violations, abuse, hatred, superiority, lording authority over people, using guilt or shame to control people, using self-pity to demand our way, or using blackmail to control people. But our fears can also motivate us, fears such as: insecurity, disloyalty, pride, loss of wealth, loss of power, loss of privileges, loss of relationship, loss of purpose, loss of satisfaction, loss of self-image, loss of happiness, loss of benefits, loss of love, and loss of self-esteem.

Scenario (V): Attempt to criticize or attack the person(s). This is meant to hurt the person(s) or take revenge on them for the injustice(s). Slander, gossip, meanness, hostility, character assassinations, malice, hatred, and yes… eventually possibly using rape, or murder, along with "I will pay them back and more…I'll teach them" are sins, attitudes, actions that make up parts of this scenario.

Some of these scenarios can lead to insanity, mental illness, depression, unhappiness, despair, and not wanting to live, and if we want to live we will seek to survive independently from God but we will become dependent on idols for our happiness, such as food, drink, sex, power, money, experiences…etc. which are all unhealthy for our souls in this context.

I personally have found myself tempted by some of these scenarios compulsively, and have often given into some of them (even though I wanted to suppress my lashing out at people). They can become real destinations that arrive so quickly when supposed or real infractions happened. I for the longest time immediately found myself in the "insensitivity" stage in the blink of an eye not knowing how I got there each time when conflict surfaced. I did not feel the bump in the road because it felt so smooth and normal to get there.

I have gone through much of my life not correctly anticipating how my words and actions would make others feel only wanting to not get into trouble and ultimately only caring about my own desires. Jesus said a person who finds his or her life will lose it, but whoever loses his or her life for Jesus' sake will find it.[81]

Question: Do I continue in selfishness or do I pursue altruism in the little intrigues of each day? I want forgiveness, but that means knowing the full extent of how I harmed others (because if I don't, then I don't know the gravity of my sins and how much I am forgiven when forgiven) and that means to know how people feel when I have hurt them. To sense how people might feel now when I do stuff helps me to ward off hurting them. I choose to be open to and pursue this reality from now on with Jesus' grace. This also helps to stop me from judging people.

Healthily Processed Anger:

For me I had to learn how to slow the process down, of getting to a place of insensitivity in the twinkle of an eye, so I could see how my "anger" went to "bad assumptions", how "bad assumptions" went to "indulging my fear"; how "my fear" went to "pride and judging"; how "pride and judging" went to "insensitivity"; and how "insensitivity" went to "trying to control" people.

I went through this process so that my prayers could be more strategic to deal with this mess (or my former way of thinking and former way of life) that I created with the devil's help.

I wanted to be able to renew and change my unhealthy mind

---

[81] Cf. Matthew 10:39

and attitudes with Jesus' help. But even when one recognizes these dynamics at work one needs a better way than the above unhealthy scenarios.

This requires undoing these habitual sin habits committed out of my human anger triggered by injustices each time, and then to deal with my broken relationships in healthy ways instead.[82] This process takes time and takes a learning curve that will see many victories that bring releases and moments of joy, but also many "seeming defeats" that are just part of the learning curve and should not be seen as failures. The defeats are part of the learning curve and not meant to squash my hope or to shame me. God will never leave us nor forsake us.

Healing Our Relationships

Judgments and condemnations never heal relationships. We need to get to a place of clean, non-toxic, gentle-caring for people, and kind energy which is reached through heartfelt honest prayer that involves confession to God, repentance, and renewing our minds.

Kindness and gentleness in listening and communicating with those in the conflict in non-threatening, non-blaming and non-shaming ways are very important to building trust. Accepting our wrongful parts in the conflict is key. Asking forgiveness, and forgiving those who hurt us are what will make our relationships go forward. Then setting boundaries

---

[82] Cf. my book Dismantling the Tree of Knowledge of Good and Evil Within So Love Can Thrive

non-threateningly (when the Holy Spirit says it is OK (not out of fear or meanness)). Setting boundaries with clean energy and peace is crucial while being open to compromise where it is wise, prudent, and full of commonsense.

Some people won't be open to this. One will sense their energy, along with walls going up from them that warn us to not push or pursue for reconciliation. When one senses this one is reading the person's energy, so respecting the person's energy, along with the person needs to be done. It is telling one that no matter what one says it will be taken as a threat, an accusation, or an attack. One is not bound to pursue the relationship with them in this case, but being kind to them and praying for healing are both wise.

Understanding that relationships are two-way-streets and that we ought not try to manipulate or control others is key to health and happiness. If need be, we may need to cut off ties with the person or party that does not want to play fair.

An Aside:

Sometimes people can be so jaded that they expect the worst from almost everyone. Their judgments are so skewed that they take the good things people do or say and twist them into something awful and choose to get offended without giving people a chance. When this operates, then fears, and feeling threatened, or being insecure can be at the root of it all. Or, it can be done out of wanting to dominate, out of pride, or out of arrogance by trying to put up a strong front; either way they land up selling people short, not trusting them, and if they voice or act out their wrongful judgments or offense they land up hurting people. Again, hardening one's heart towards people caught in these ways is unhealthy.

PART V

16 LIVING OUT OF GRACE VS. A SLAVE AND LAW MENTALITY

An untrusting person cannot receive love fully. If they know the boundaries of acceptance in an important relationship they will hold onto the boundaries as tightly as possible and somehow try to survive by keeping the rules. This is slave-like and parasitical in nature. People like this relate more to the boundaries or rules than to the actual person they are in relationship with. They play it safe. But there is good news, one doesn't need to hang onto such boundaries of acceptance and safety to function any longer when it comes to relationships. The fear of not doing so can evaporate.

It is not fear of the boundaries that keeps a relationship intact and healthy, but freely giving and receiving of love that determine the health of the relationship and its boundaries.

The thing is that often those who despise weakness in others, desire strength in those who are weak. But trying to be strong because someone else desires it does not work for many reasons. It only works when we realize we want to be strong, and to do it for that reason.

People who are rule focused are so because they often have unresolved trauma, rejection, or conflict (think: being attacked) somewhere in the past. My book: *Dismantling the*

Tree of Knowledge of Good and Evil Within So Love can Thrive has some healthy strategies on how to tackle such issues.

God sees being strong as healthy, and also those who practice it. Healthy practices are good. Trying to be strong because others desire it amounts to "people pleasing" and is motivated by fear and does not work.

When we learn to love and connect with the person instead of being rule focused. We also start to determine the shape of the relationship as our partner has been doing all along[83]. It is no longer a lopsided creative adventure or nightmare. We begin to seek playing it safe less so and instead get stronger as time goes by in our relating and identity. This is a gradual learning curve. It is healthy to embrace this way of relating.

To remain confident (or strong) I choose to see my confidence as part of my identity in Jesus Christ. I'm not dependent on continual interpretations of events, or repeatedly winning arguments with the devil to be confident about my present and future relational life.

Healthy Love Relationships

What is a 100:100 relationship as opposed to a 50:50 relationship?[84]

A 100:100 relationship means both partners give 100% and aren't needy in a weak way. They want to be together because they are attracted to each other's personalities,

---

[83] This thought comes from my friend Vicky
[84] Idea originates from a friend

make ups, goals, relating, strengths, and caring.

A 50:50 relationship means there is neediness from both partners in the relationship with both trying to meet each other's neediness. By neediness I mean that there is weakness in each person. They don't ever seek and find healing for their neediness instead they feel happy they are needed and that their partners console and comfort them in their respective weaknesses.

This does not mean there is no giving and receiving in a 100:100 relationship, there is. Instead there are often roles in sharing the common work load and household duties. They are dependent on each other but in a positive way not a needy way.

The goal of any healthy relationship is to make each other aim at and be mature, lacking nothing.

In an unhealthy relationship it means the partners are aiding and using the weaknesses of each other to find security. And they misunderstand this as love. But healthy love in a relationship always raises people up, gives them dignity, and helps them go further and higher in their journey together than before[85]. The goal of any healthy relationship is to become strong and not needy.

Whether our partner is a spouse, a friend or an institution the same applies.

---

[85] Cf. James 1:4, and Colossians 2:10

PART IV

17 HOW LOVE PLAYS OUT IN WHO GOD IS

The Bible says that God is one, and some people wrongly take this to mean that He is one person. To believe this one would have to say for all eternity past before God created the world or anything in it, that He was turned into Himself in love since there was nothing else to love back then besides Himself, because He is love. Since God is perfect, that would mean that self-love was the greatest good back then. Since God can't improve His character, that would mean that self-love would still be the greatest good even after God created us in His own image. And that would mean that selfishness is what we all ought to aim for.

Put another way, when God created us in His own image He intended us to become like Him in our way of relating. Since God does not change, that would mean that the highest goal or objective we could have is self-love. If this were the case, then selfishness would be considered a virtue. And God could therefore not be called Love in the sense that some of us know him (this) today. But Jesus said that the greatest love we could have is to lay down our lives for our friends. Therefore, God can't only be one person, because if He were He would have to be a selfish God. It therefore doesn't make sense to believe in a God who is only one person.

Christianity on the other hand has rightly taught from Scripture and Tradition that God consists of three persons. Because this is so, these three persons are turned outwards towards each other in Love for all eternity (past, present, and future). This fellowship was rained on, mocked, and laughed at, on the cross. Jesus did not feel united with God the Father during His passion but He was because God cannot be divided. At the cross the Trinity suffered together the ridiculing of men in order to bring men into the Trinity's holy (healthy) community. It is this kind of community that the world lacks. Followers of Jesus are commissioned to bring the life of this community to everyone by partaking of it themselves and sharing it. They are commissioned to love according to the life that is in the Trinity. The Trinity never abandons any of its persons; but they chose to become vulnerable so that they could win us back, even if that looked like God the Father abandoned Jesus, which He never would do. God was in Christ Jesus on the cross reconciling the world to Himself.

ABOUT THE AUTHOR

I lived my early life in South Africa, but have lived since then in Canada. I have struggled with Schizophrenia since 1992. I have struggled with many addictions. I am fighting the fight of faith. For more information or to contact me go to www.brokenintofreedom.ca

BOOKS BY THE AUTHOR

Exploring Faith, Hope & Love
Dismantling the Tree of Knowledge of Good and Evil Within
So Love Can Thrive
Exploring Humility and Pride
Going Deeper With the Twelve Steps
To Be Broken into Freedom: A Spiritual Journey

Made in the USA
Monee, IL
24 August 2019